The Spring of Hope

Sermons for the Seasons of Faith

— DOUGLAS DALES —

Douglas Dales

Sacristy
Press

Sacristy Press
PO Box 612, Durham, DH1 9HT

www.sacristy.co.uk

First published in 2021 by Sacristy Press, Durham.

Sacristy Limited, registered in England & Wales, number 7565667

British Library Cataloguing-in-Publication Data
A catalogue record for the book is available from the British Library

ISBN 978-1-78959-173-6

For our beloved grandchildren

Non Angli sed Angeli

With Thee is the well of life: and in Thy light shall we see light.
Psalm 36:9

Contents

Preface

These reflections on the Christian Year comprise material prepared by me to support online worship provided during the closure of churches in 2020 for our rural benefice of eight parishes in Berkshire. Some of them were first delivered to the nuns at Fairacres in Oxford and those at Wantage; one was delivered at Marlborough College where I was Chaplain. Some saints' days have been included within the seasonal material. Bible references are drawn either from the Revised Version or from the Revised English Bible. Passages cited from the writings of saints have been translated by me.

Douglas Dales
Candlemas 2021

PART 1

Advent

The Presence of the Lord

"Lord Jesus Christ, Son of the Living God, have mercy upon me."

The roots of this ancient prayer, the Jesus Prayer, lie deep in the Old Testament, in the story to which Exodus 3 alludes, the revealing of the Holy Name of God to Moses at the Burning Bush: "I AM THAT I AM" (Exodus 3:14). The name of the Lord—*Yahweh*—is a transliteration of this Name as it appears in the Hebrew scripture, written without vowels because it is too holy for direct pronunciation by Jews in the synagogue to this day. By the time of Jesus, there was a solemn celebration in the Temple at Jerusalem of the Holy Name as the symbol of God's covenant with Israel and of their indissoluble bond with him. In the Acts of the Apostles, as elsewhere in the New Testament, the Name of Jesus is a saving name: "In the Name of Jesus Christ of Nazareth, whom you crucified, whom God raised from the dead, in him (*or* in this Name) does this person stand here before you whole" (Acts 4:10). The promise to Joseph and Mary was that the child to be born would be called Jesus: "for it is he that shall save his people from their sins" (Matthew 1:21).

For Christians, the Jesus Prayer, as it has come to be called, widely used throughout the Orthodox Church, is not a meditative mantra: it is a solemn and loving invocation of the One whose presence is real and immediate. It is a personal response to the self-revelation of God in Jesus, who stoops to save us from our sins, and who by this prayer enables us to receive within ourselves his divine inbreathing, the gift of his Holy Spirit. This prayer springs from the Trinitarian reality of God himself: it is a sharing in the *koinonia* or communion that lies at the heart of God, Father, Son and Holy Spirit.

The Greek word *koinonia* is a powerful clue, because there is a profound connection between the Jesus Prayer and the Eucharist. Both are part of the *communio sanctorum*—the communion of saints or the communion in holy realities, the Latin can mean either or probably both. This ancient prayer has a long lineage within the monastic life of the Eastern Church. It can be traced back at least as far as the sixth century and, in the Western tradition, the emphasis that Benedict placed upon repeated repetition of the words with which the Divine Office opens—"O God, make speed to save us; O Lord, make haste to help us"—looks back to the practice of the earliest Egyptian monks as recorded by Cassian. The practice of the Jesus Prayer is therefore never a solitary or individual exercise: it is a participation in the continual prayer of the Church, across time and space, and a preparation for the deep mystery of the Eucharist, which lies at the heart of the Church's life. Consider for a moment how it illuminates each step of the Eucharistic pilgrimage of faith and worship.

The opening Collect for Purity, which has been in the English rite since Anglo-Saxon times, and was probably written by Alcuin, chimes exactly with opening of the heart to God in the Jesus Prayer, as we invoke the mercy of Jesus: "Almighty God, to whom all hearts are open, all desires known, and from whom no secrets are hidden". Alcuin used to pray with outstretched arms: "Lord Jesus Christ, Son of the Living God, in your Name I lift up my hands."

"*Kyrie eleison*" provides another direct link, and indeed can be used as a variant form of the Jesus Prayer: "*Kyrie Jesu, Christe eleison; Christe Jesu, Kyrie eleison.*" The root of the word *eleison* is to do with anointing with olive oil: this therefore is a prayer for healing and for anointing by the Holy Spirit. First and foremost, however, these are prayers of penitence—"Lord, have mercy upon us sinners." But they are also prayers of loyalty and devotion, for Jesus is the Lord of our lives.

The *Gloria in Excelsis* addresses God the Father, and also Jesus as Lord. Its language contains the message of Christmas, the mystery of the incarnation; and part of that good news was the giving of the Name of Jesus, as we have heard in our Gospel today. It reminds us that the Jesus Prayer is an acclamation of love, joy and worship. It is kneeling with the shepherds and the holy parents of Jesus at the crib, taking the child Jesus into the arms of our prayer: the Jesus Prayer becomes a cradling whisper of love to a child—the message of Francis of Assisi.

The daily practice of the Jesus Prayer is also a sanctification of time. Following the example of Ignatius Loyola, there is no reason why the Collect for each week cannot be used to illuminate some aspect of the earthly life of Jesus or of his teaching and associated with use of this prayer. For the language of the Jesus Prayer is drawn directly from the way people addressed Jesus in the Gospels: it is the prayer of the leper, the outcast, the thief dying beside him on the cross. But it is also the prayer of the resurrection, because the Jesus we address is the living Lord: the prayer is the awed response of Mary Magdalene and of Thomas: "My Lord and my God!" (John 20:28).

Chapter 20 of John's Gospel closes with this statement: "These things are written so that you may believe that Jesus is the Christ, the Son of God, and that believing you may have life in his Name" (John 20:31). The Jesus Prayer is an epitome of these words, an expression of belief; and in Christianity this word means both faith and trust: it is the Creed in miniature.

It can also be an act of intercession. It is often very hard to prevent other thoughts from intruding into meditative prayer; but when they involve other people, they can certainly be turned into intercession for them—even for our enemies. The Jesus Prayer can, of course, conclude with the word "us" rather than "me"; and it makes a very fine framework for regular intercessions, private or corporate.

In the end, both the Jesus Prayer and the consecration of the Eucharist bring us to the threshold of the eternal reality of heaven, to participation in the worship of the angels, and the communion of the saints with God the Trinity. We invoke the Name of God in the words of the *Sanctus*, and we acclaim the entry of Jesus into human history in the words of the *Benedictus*. We celebrate the divine self-giving, we commemorate Calvary, and we look for the coming of God's kingdom. Perhaps the oldest known Aramaic Christian prayer points the way: "*Maranatha*" (1 Corinthians 16:22). This prayer—"Our Lord comes" or "Come, Lord"—is very close in spirit to the Jesus Prayer, expressing the sense of the *parousia*—the presence of the risen Christ at the heart of the Church's life.

That heart is found at the altar of the Eucharist where the life of the Church is constituted. It is also found in our hearts: "Do you not know that your body is a sanctuary of the Holy Spirit who is within you, which you have received from God?" (1 Corinthians 6:19). The Jesus Prayer is a prayer of the heart, prayer within the sanctuary of the heart; a prayer of self-emptying and self-offering upon the altar of the heart. It is very close in spirit to devotion to the Sacred Heart of Jesus. For as a child once said: "Heaven is a very big place because it is where God is; but the way to it is very small because it is in our heart."

2

The Challenge of Advent

It is too easy to ignore the parts of the Gospels, such as Mark 13, where Jesus spoke to his disciples about the coming end of the age. But for the first generation of those who heard and remembered him, his predictions about the fate of the holy city of Jerusalem and its Temple loomed large. Within the lifetime of many of these people, the terrible events that Jesus predicted came to pass, as Jerusalem was besieged and sacked by the Romans in AD 70, and its Temple destroyed after a failed revolution and a bloody war. This momentous event was the indirect catalyst many centuries later for the creation of the state of Israel in the aftermath of the Second World War, so it is part of modern history too. The site of the Temple is now occupied by a great and beautiful mosque, and Jerusalem remains still a potential flashpoint, as the focal point of three world religions, Judaism, Christianity and Islam.

The memory of what Jesus said about the Temple, and the division he caused within the Jewish religion, was further embittered by the destruction of the Temple and beginning of the exile of the Jews from their ancestral land. At the time he spoke, no one could envisage the destruction of so splendid a centre of Jewish faith and worship, to which pilgrims came from far and wide. Nonetheless currents of violent opposition to Roman rule were swirling, in the lifetime of Jesus and immediately afterwards, that would precipitate war by their acts of religiously inspired terrorism against Roman occupation. The destruction of Jesus himself only makes sense within this context of fear and repression. Was he also a false Messiah?

In his resurrection, Jesus privately warned those closest to him that his way as Messiah was not the way of violence and revolution. Instead he predicted persecution and ostracism from the synagogue and Temple for many of his Jewish followers. "The gospel must first be preached to all nations", however. The scope of his mission was universal, breaking out of the narrow confines of Judaism, while fulfilling its hope of a Redeemer. His prediction of the siege and fall of the holy city was stark, and what he said came true, recorded by the Jewish historian Josephus. The Romans erected a temple of their own on the site of the Temple—"an abomination of desolation" indeed.

This sense of impending crisis loomed over Jewish society and religion as people feared a terrible outcome. In times of conflict, of chronic insecurity and fear, human beings often sense a deeper dimension in what is happening, recognizing that a crisis is indeed a moment of judgement, which is what the word "crisis" means in Greek. The temptation to reach out for simplistic solutions, conspiracy theories, to seek scapegoats, or to succumb to the blandishments of gurus and charismatic political or religious leadership can become compelling; there are many examples of this tendency throughout history and also at the present time. Jesus warns his disciples in every generation to be on their guard against such delusions and deceptions, however plausible they may appear to be.

It has been tempting for many years to ignore completely what the New Testament has to say about the end of the world as we know it. Now, with the great crisis of ecology, change has to come to consumer capitalism across the world. Will it come peacefully and how should it be approached? At its root, there is a deep confusion of values, which springs from living in the world as if God does not exist: but this is his world, not ours. Yet human rapacity is destroying the natural environment and inflicting poverty on millions of people. The situation is being made far worse in the immediate term by the global impact of the present pandemic. Lack of belief in God results in a chronic confusion of goals.

The word "end" can have two meanings, both of which are evident in the New Testament. There is the sense of finishing, bringing to an end in that sense. But there is also the sense of "end" as the goal, in Greek *telos*, as the fulfilment of divine purpose. In times of crisis, of war and persecution, this perspective can loom large, as people sense that the purposes of God cannot be ignored without penalty. You can no more ignore the law of divine love than you can ignore the law of gravity. In lurid ways, many disaster movies express this foreboding.

Embedded in this dramatic Gospel passage, however, are some key words, which hint at how this divine end is being achieved. "Travail" is a word associated with childbirth. It also captures the momentous forces by which the earth as we know it was created and is still being formed. "Endurance" is another key word, reminding us that today's crisis has antecedents, and that there is a future for humanity if it returns to God. "Forewarned" is another key word, signifying that God's purpose has been revealed in Christ for those who seriously seek it and order their lives accordingly. There is no need for panic or gloom among Christians, simply active repentance. Just as people spot the coming of spring when buds begin to break on a fig tree or any tree, so it is possible to discern the hidden pattern to human history, which has its focal point in the person of Jesus Christ.

The way of Christ alters for ever the sense of time. Instead of an eternal cycle without meaning, or an endless procession of events, human history is revealed as the crucial theatre for human choice, for good or ill, always a moment of opportunity. For Christians, "the end" does not simply mean the end of things as we know it, though this is certainly part of Christian belief, reminding each of us that in the end we shall have to give an account for how we have lived and acted before Christ, who will be our judge. "The end" also means the hidden goal, the centre around which our lives may circle in a deepening spiral of engagement with God, as he comes to us in the person of Christ. His life, death and resurrection is the point where divine and eternal reality engages with the process of time and history, holding out a choice to each human generation and each person, which for some will be life-giving, but for others destructive. God's "hour" steals upon us often unawares, most notably at times of grave illness and impending death, but also in times of social crisis and conflict.

So what should we do? Jesus commands us to "Watch and pray, for you do not know when the time is." Christians are called to watch for the coming of the Lord, not just at the end of things, or in the midst of a crisis, but in hidden ways day by day. Will he find us asleep, or so preoccupied with our busy lives as to be oblivious to his presence among us? "*Maranatha!*" is one of the oldest prayers in Christianity, and it means 'Be present with us, Lord.' It is a prayer that encapsulates the mystery of

Christ's presence in the Eucharist, and in all moments of hidden prayer when we seek him with our whole heart, "in the evening, at mid-night, at dawn or in the morning". We will have a better sense of what "the end" means if we make Christ the hidden centre of our lives now, for that is our vocation as Christians.

3

The Kiss of Peace

One of the privileges of a priest is to be expected to read some of the psalms every day at Morning and Evening Prayer. The *Book of Common Prayer* arranges them so that a person can say them once each month. In monasteries, psalms constitute the core framework of prayers by day and night. Why is this so, and how should we read or sing the psalms?

The psalms connect us first and foremost with the Jewish faith from which Christianity sprang and to which it owes so much. When we pray the psalms, we pray with our Jewish brothers and sisters, and we affirm their faith and worship too. Some of the devotional poetry and prayers in Islam also have their roots in the psalms and other poetical parts of the Bible. So there is a bond of prayer with Muslims as well. Familiarity with the psalms provides a sure way into the spirit of the Old Testament: their poetic language provides a key with which to unlock its meaning. Praying the psalms also reminds us of our fellowship with Christians who have gone before us, as well as all those who use them across the world in their prayers and worship today. In the early Church, and also in the Middle Ages, Christians learnt to read through memorizing the psalms, often in their musical expression, and so the language of the psalms became the vocabulary of their thought and prayer. Plainsong and Anglican psalm chants are examples of this rich tradition of worship.

For Christians, the psalms are first and foremost the prayers of Jesus himself, in the sense that he would have used them every day as a devout Jew, privately and also at worship in the synagogue. As he was dying on the cross, words from the psalms were on his lips. Medieval psalters often gloss the Hebrew titles of the psalms with pointers as to how a psalm might connect with moments in the life and sufferings of our Lord, or of his apostles and saints. In this way, the psalms have become the heartbeat of the Church. The range of their expression, the human dilemmas and difficulties to which they give voice, become an insight into the real experience of Jesus as a human being in dialogue with God his Father: "My God, my God, why have you forsaken me?" (Psalm 22:1). As the use of the psalms in prayer enlarges our own sympathy, it also draws us alongside others who are suffering temptation and difficulty in their lives now. For the heartbeat of the Church is the heartbeat of Christ in his love for humanity, lost in its sins, and so often cut off from any sense of God's presence and love. As an example, how may Psalm 85 be read by Christians in the light of the coming of Christ?

> Lord, thou art become gracious unto thy land: thou hast turned
> away the captivity of Jacob.

Christians think back to the great story of the Exodus and later of the return of God's people from exile to their holy city of Jerusalem. Despite all the trauma of history, God's purpose was working itself out until Christ himself came, "full of grace and truth".

> Thou hast forgiven the offence of thy people: and covered all
> their sins.

Christ came into the world to bear away the sins of humanity, to cover their toxic legacy with his own blood, shed on the cross. Forgiveness stands at the heart of the gospel, in the teaching and healing miracles of Jesus, as well as in his prayer for his enemies as he was dying: "Father, forgive them for they know not what they do."

> Thou hast turned away all thy displeasure: and turned thyself
> from thy wrathful indignation.

Christ came into the world to demonstrate the loving purpose of God towards human beings, and to end the alienation that stood as a barrier between each person and God himself. In his own person Jesus absorbed the full force of divine rejection of all that is evil, and which destroys human beings as well as the created world.

> Turn us then, O God our Saviour: and let thine anger cease from us.

Christians are called to a long road of repentance, like the Prodigal Son, who woke up to the fact that he was lost, having squandered his inheritance and was now in the grip of evil oppression. He returned to his Father and was welcomed home as a beloved son, for Christ came to seek and to save the lost.

> Wilt thou be displeased at us for ever: and wilt thou stretch out
> thy wrath from one generation to another?

These words express the heartfelt regret of many human beings as they reflect on their personal history and on the manifold injustices and evils that we perpetrate on each other. Yet the crises of history, of war or pandemic, may jolt us into a more honest sense of who we are and to whom this world belongs. For we cannot ignore the sovereignty of God for very long without a collision with reality.

> Wilt thou not turn again and quicken us: that thy people may
> rejoice in thee?

It is the distinctive vocation and capacity of human beings to ask the question "Why?". A notable example in the Bible is Job. The bottom fell out of his life, he lost everything that he valued. His friends tried to console him and offer him explanations. But in the end, it was only when he confronted God, or rather allowed himself to be confronted by God, that his questions were heard. Jesus said that he came into the world to offer "life in all its fullness", but on God's terms, not ours.

> Show us thy mercy, O Lord: and grant us thy salvation.

Surely this prayer is the hidden heart of Advent. "Lord Jesus Christ, Son of the Living God, have mercy on me, a sinner." The words of this ancient prayer, which constitute the inner spirit of Eastern Orthodox monastic life, sum up what needs to happen in our own lives if we are to draw near to Christ, who draws near to us in his perpetual coming among us.

> I will hearken what the Lord God will say concerning me: for
> he shall speak peace unto his people, and to his saints, that they
> turn not again.

What does the Risen Christ say to his friends and disciples? "Peace be with you." But as he says this, he shows them the wounds in his hands and feet. "Peace" in Hebrew means complete wellbeing, healing and wholeness. But it comes at a price because it flows from the cross of Christ. We have to accept that "in his will is our peace". That is a hard road to follow.

> For his salvation is nigh them that fear him: that glory may dwell
> in our land.

In Christ, God comes near to us. The question is how near we are to him. Are we facing in the right direction, or is our back to the light as we contemplate our own shadow? The fear of the Lord means a constant sense of his presence—and also of his love. In those who seek him with their whole heart each day, his glory can be at home and shine through them: for his glory shines from the face of Jesus Christ into the depths of our hearts.

> Mercy and truth are met together: righteousness and peace have
> kissed each other.

These lovely words sum up the mystery and beauty of the gospel. No wonder that Jesus bade his disciples to read the psalms in order to discern the meaning of his coming. Truth is tempered by mercy, as we see so often in the Gospel stories of how Jesus dealt with people who came to him. God's righteousness finds its expression in him, and his healing embrace pours the peace of God into the hearts of men, women and children.

> Truth shall flourish out of the earth: and righteousness hath
> looked down from heaven.

These words have always been associated in Christianity with the coming of Jesus into the world in the womb of the Blessed Virgin Mary, as "the Word became flesh". They may also be associated with the Baptism and Transfiguration of Jesus, acclaimed by God as "my beloved Son, in whom I am well pleased". But they may also be associated with ourselves inasmuch as it is God's loving purpose that his Word should make its home within us as his children, so that his truth may be expressed within the fragility of our human nature, made from the dust of the earth.

> Yea, the Lord shall show loving-kindness: and our land shall give
> her increase.

These words remind us that the loving purpose of God embraces the whole of creation and not just human beings set within it. But do we embrace the created world as we should, or do we abuse it? This is one of the big questions of our time: what is the goal, the end of our society? Will it bring about its own destruction, its end? Can it change its ways and its values?

> Righteousness shall go before him: and he shall direct his going
> in the way.

Another way of translating the Hebrew of this closing verse speaks of how God will set our steps in his way, for Jesus said, "I am the way, the truth, and the life: no-one can come to God the Father except through me." This is the challenge of Advent: for in the words of Jesus, "How narrow is the path and how afflicted is the way that leads to life; and how few are they who find it"! Human beings cannot have peace without righteousness as found in Christ. In the words of Augustine, commenting on this psalm: "These two, righteousness and peace, love one another and kiss one another, so that a person who is righteous may find peace by kissing righteousness." Or in the words of Bonaventure, commenting on the story of the Prodigal Son: "In Christ is accomplished the union of the most sublime love and the mutual embrace of two natures, whereby God kisses us, and we kiss God."

4

The Mystery of Advent

Maranatha

Whenever we come across words in Aramaic preserved in the New Testament, we should prick up our ears, as they connect us with the earliest followers of Jesus, to whom he preached in this vernacular language. The New Testament was written for Greek-speaking Jews and their Gentile converts. So when these texts preserve untranslated Aramaic words, they are significant. For example, the words Jesus used to raise the daughter of Jairus from certain death are in Aramaic; so too are some of the dying words of Jesus on the cross, taken from Psalm 22. When Paul refers in his letters to the Romans and Galatians to praying to God as "Abba—Father", he probably has the Lord's Prayer in mind. Perhaps for later Christians like ourselves, the little prayer that is embedded at the very end of Paul's first letter to the church of Corinth is most striking and significant: "*Maranatha*" (1 Corinthians 16:22). Paul concludes his letter by citing it as he signed off personally, commending his hearers to the love and grace of Christ.

What does this Aramaic prayer "*Maranatha*" mean? Fortunately it is translated for us at the very end of the book of Revelation: "Come, Lord Jesus!" In both passages, it seems to be set in a formal dialogue of loving prayer, something rooted in the worship of the earliest Jewish Christian Church. Perhaps the meaning of this dialogue of love is expressed at the end of Paul's second letter to Corinth in the familiar words: "The grace of the Lord Jesus Christ, and the love of God, and the communion of the Holy Spirit be with you all." This impression of worship and fellowship is confirmed by the other place where this Aramaic prayer is preserved: in a text called *The Didache*. This was composed as the New Testament was being completed, and it contains the Lord's Prayer, and also the earliest extant prayer for consecrating bread and wine at the Eucharist. Here are some words from this lovely consecrating prayer:

> We give you thanks, our holy Father, for your holy Name which you have made to dwell within our hearts, and for the faith and life and knowledge that you have made known to us through Jesus, your servant [or child]; to you be glory for ever.
>
> As this broken bread was once scattered upon the mountains and then was gathered up and became one, so may your Church be gathered together from the ends of the earth into your kingdom; for yours is the glory and power through Jesus Christ for ever.
>
> May grace come and this world pass away. Hosanna to the God of David! If anyone is holy, let him approach: but if anyone is not holy, repent! Maranatha! Amen.

So the reference point for the prayer, *Maranatha*, is to be found in the Eucharist, the service which defines the existence of the Church in every place and generation, and which has been celebrated ever since the time of Jesus. Why is this so? It is because the Eucharist stands at the heart of Christianity, and in it, Christians sense the reality of the Risen Jesus as he gives himself in the bread and wine, which become his Body and Blood. In the Eucharist, we look back to the coming of Jesus in history and forward to the coming of his kingdom. We also look outwards to other human beings, within and beyond the Church; and we also look inwards to deepen our personal relationship with Christ through prayer and love.

"Come, Lord Jesus!" Note that we address Jesus as the historic person described for us in the Gospel. This is why reading the Gospels each day should be the foundation of our Christian life. We can only know Jesus truly as a person if we do so; but we shall find that no Gospel ever sums up all that he was and is. Their genius conveys the keen sense of his person in a way that changes our lives over time. As a prayer expressing the heart of the mystery of the Eucharist, "*Maranatha*" still colours the language of our worship: "The Lord is here: his Spirit is with us", and "Christ has died, Christ is risen, Christ will come again."

"Come, Lord Jesus!" also points us forward to the coming of God's kingdom, in words that we find in the Lord's Prayer: 'Thy kingdom come, Thy will be done.' In the third part of the consecrating prayer of the Eucharist, we not only remember the coming of Christ in history but also his coming at the end of all things to usher in the kingdom of God. We do not know what form this end will take, but we know that 'end' means the fulfilment of God's eternal purpose, and that the key to this is the person of Christ, by whom all human beings are and will be judged.

"Come, Lord Jesus!" is a prayer for others as well as for ourselves. It is a prayer for the world's need, and for the rolling back of the dark shadow of evil and suffering that disfigures human society and damages the created world. "Give us this day our daily bread" are words that we say each time we use the Lord's Prayer. At the simplest level these are words of gratitude, like grace at mealtimes. They also remind us that we should share bread with others, especially with those in need. "Fruit of the earth and work of human hands: may it become for us the bread of life." In these words, is a whole theology of ecology.

The prayer "*Maranatha*" was also a prayer within the context of Christian fellowship and love, and the Lord's Prayer addresses this too. "By this will people know that you are truly my disciples if you love one another, as I have loved you—even loving your enemies." This sums up the teaching of Jesus in the Gospels, teaching backed up by his own example even when he was dying. In Matthew's version of the Lord's Prayer, the words for "our daily bread" mean "our bread from your kingdom". This reminds us that Jesus said, "I am the Bread of life—the living bread that came down from heaven." This is why the Lord's Prayer is our response to the consecrating prayer of the Eucharist.

"Come, Lord Jesus!" is a prayer that directs us inward to our own personal love of Jesus Christ, for he says, "Behold, I stand at the door and knock: if a person hears my voice and opens the door, I will come into him and will eat with him, and he with me." There is a vivid and moving example of this happening at the end of Luke's Gospel when the disciples invite the stranger Jesus into their home at Emmaus. Many of the other resurrection appearances of Jesus also occur in the context of a meal.

"Come Lord Jesus!" is perhaps best expressed in the ancient Jesus Prayer, used widely in the Orthodox Church, and which dates back as far as the third or fourth century. Its words echo the way in which people responded to Jesus in the Gospels: "Lord Jesus Christ, Son of the Living God, have mercy upon me, a sinner." This simple prayer opens the door of the heart to the coming of Christ in a deeply personal way. It can also be used as a prayer of penitence and intercession—"upon us sinners"; or as a prayer for others—"for our family", "for our children", "for those in need", or "for someone". It is a prayer for quiet meditation. It is also a fine prayer of preparation for Holy Communion, or before reading the Gospel privately. It conveys to us something of the immediacy and mystery of the Aramaic original, *Maranatha*, and so it links us with the earliest generation of Christians. It is a prayer, like the Lord's Prayer itself, that unites us with the communion of saints on earth and in heaven, whose prayer is eternally, "Thy kingdom come, Thy will be done—*Maranatha*—Come Lord Jesus!"

5

Magnificat

*"My spirit has rejoiced in God my Saviour: for He has
looked upon the humility of his handmaiden."*

These memorable words in Luke 1:46 enshrine the mystery of Mary
the Mother of the Lord—the *Theotokos*—the God-bearer, for it is her
vocation to lead us deeper into the mystery of Christ himself. In the
pattern of her humility may be traced the passion of his humanity. In
her response is the guide to our own discipleship, called as she was to
respond to God with the words, "Behold, the servant of the Lord: be it
unto me according to your word" (Luke 1:38).

She was hailed by Gabriel as "endued with grace, for the Lord is with
you". It is interesting to note how closely the language of the prologue of
John's Gospel shadows this story: for example in the words, "for of his
fullness have we all received, grace poured upon grace", words which echo
the language of the psalms: "You are fairer than the children of men; grace
is poured into your lips: therefore God has blessed you for ever" (Psalm
45:2). These words could apply equally to Mary or to Jesus, and from
ancient times this psalm has been associated with her commemoration.
In many ways, the prologue of John's Gospel is an extended meditation
upon the meaning and nature of the nativity of our Lord, for he was born
"not of blood, nor of the will of the flesh, nor of the will of man, but of
God". Now he gives that right, capacity and power to those who believe
in him. Yet how can this be?

In the New Testament, the Greek word for humility—*tapeinosis*—has
the sense of humiliation as well as of humility, of lowly social status as
well as self-abasement; it can also mean chastisement, and it is closely
associated with the fragility of human bodily existence, created from the

dust of the ground, as the Latin word *humilitas* indicates, being derived from the word for earth—*humus*.

The social humility and obscurity of Mary and her family is not in doubt: as Ignatius of Antioch said in his letter to the Ephesians, "The virginity of Mary and her giving birth were hidden from the ruler of this age, as was also the death of the Lord—three mysteries to be loudly proclaimed now, yet which were accomplished in the silence of God." It is surely Mary's own authority that is hinted at in the two references in Luke's nativity narrative to how she "treasured these things—words and deeds—and pondered them in her heart". For as Paul said, "God chose the foolish things of the world to put to shame the wise, and the weak things of the world to put to shame the strong; and base things that are despised, even things that are not, to bring to nothing the things that are" (1 Corinthians 1:27). Was this perhaps his reflection on the mystery of the Incarnation at the root of Christianity?

Mary's humility reflected also the "down to earth" and humble moral character of her family, and also the love and loyalty of her fiancé, Joseph. Without their support, the safe birth of Jesus could never have occurred in Bethlehem. This is a story of human faithfulness, of love and courage in the face of potential social hostility and misunderstanding. In her day, a girl counted for little in herself: she was either her father's daughter or her husband's wife. To become pregnant before marriage ran the risk of being socially ostracized, as Matthew's account of Joseph's dilemma makes quite clear. So Mary's child-bearing was a hidden, and perhaps not so hidden, humiliation, to which Joseph responded with amazing faith, generosity and loyalty, for a girl who was pregnant in this way was a disaster, and liable to be stoned to death. Even if she were married, she would carry a stigma for the rest of her life, as would her child, for in such a close-knit society word spread, and rumour embellished it, as is perhaps echoed later in the reproach to Jesus: "Where is your father then? . . . at least we were not born of fornication!" (John 8:41).

Mary's humiliation continued when their own son seemed to repudiate his parents in the Temple in response to her words, "Son, why have you behaved like this towards us? Look, your father and I have been looking for you full of sorrow" (Luke 2:48). This child was different—how would he turn out? There is another echo of this occasional tension in the story of Jesus at the wedding at Cana in Galilee: "Woman, what have I to do with you? My hour has not yet come" (John 2:4). Yet she commanded the servants "to do whatever he tells you to do". Then there was the terrible moment when the family put pressure on her to get Jesus to give up his embarrassing ministry, insinuating that he was mad and quite out of line. He seemed to repudiate them at one level: "Who is my mother and my brethren?" Then looking at those around him, he declared, "Behold, my mother and my brethren! For whoever shall do the will of God, that person is my brother and sister and mother" (Mark 3:34). The confusion was deeply humiliating, personally and socially, to Mary and to her family, even if at another level the words of Jesus actually affirmed the unique obedience of his own mother to the will of God. In her heart, she could not dispute the very truth she had taught him by her own word and example. But it was a costly and perplexing truth as she "went forth to him outside the camp, bearing his reproach" (Hebrews 13:13). Yet as he taught elsewhere, "how narrow is the gate and afflicted the path that leads to life, and they are few indeed who find it" (Matthew 7:14).

Mary's initial response to the angel was surely the consequence of her life of prayer and piety, nurtured by her family in the synagogue and in her home. She was a true daughter of Israel, for only those who are faithful and self-abasing before God can sense the presence of angels. Her vocation and response were also those of a young person—a teenager, in fact, as was that of Joseph as well. God was already at home in her heart before Jesus became incarnate within her. Her humility attracted the humble God, for as Augustine said, "Proud man can only be saved by the humble God." The result of such obedience and faith is expressed in one of the deepest messages of the Song of Songs: "Set me as a seal upon your heart, for love is strong as death . . . many waters cannot quench love, nor can the floods drown it" (Song of Songs 8:6). This awesome truth was put to the bitterest test by Mary's witnessing the torture by crucifixion of her own son, surely every parent's nightmare: in his beginning was his end. For at the most joyful moment of their lives, when these young parents brought their first-born son to the Temple for the purification of the mother, and to dedicate their beloved child to God in thanksgiving, Mary's destiny was revealed as entwined with that of Jesus, in life and in death: "Yea and a sword will pierce through your own soul too" (Luke

2:35). Shortly after his birth she and Joseph had had to flee for their lives with their child, becoming refugees in Egypt. Only John's Gospel records the grim fact that "there standing by the cross of Jesus was his mother and his mother's sister", and also the fact that in his extremity Jesus remembered Mary and commended her to the care of one of his closest disciples. This was the moment of her deepest chastisement—another dimension to the dark humiliation that she shared with her son.

Yet out of these close encounters with the mysterious grace of God, of living through dying, there flowed great joy, as her words at the beginning of the Magnificat indicate: "My spirit has rejoiced in God my Saviour." Her life proves the truth that Paul also discovered as a result of his own narrow and afflicted way of the cross:

> If God is for us, who can be against us? He who spared not his own
> Son, but delivered him up for us all, how shall he not also with
> him freely give us all things? Who shall separate us from the love
> of Christ? Shall tribulation, or anguish, or persecution, or famine,
> or nakedness, or peril, or the sword? No, in all these things we
> are more than conquerors through him who loved us: for I am
> persuaded that nothing in all creation shall be able to separate us
> from the love of God, which is in Christ Jesus our Lord.
>
> *Romans 8:31–39*

Mary also "spared not her own Son", yet she never deserted him. For her it was "in all these things" that she embraced him, in his life and in his death, as Michelangelo's great Pieta in St Peter's basilica in Rome portrays. It is her vulnerability that draws us close to the hidden presence of the vulnerable but life-giving love of Christ, whom we are called to embrace in humble compassion, sensitivity and love. For their presence together may be discovered in the darkest places of suffering and betrayal as well as in the poverty and affliction of human beings everywhere. Do we see their faces in them, or do we pass them by?

6

Light and Life

The Light shines in the darkness and the darkness
has never mastered or quenched it.

John 1:5

It is a lamentable fact that once again within a hundred years we are confronted globally with an ideology of nihilism: Communism, Nazism and now Islamic terrorism all have a common thread of cruelty and ruthlessness, a cult of violence and death. They have each persecuted Christianity with venom, as we can see happening today. Whatever their particular political, economic and religious causes, the flagrant proliferation of systematic atrocity brings into sharp relief the contrast and collision between moral and spiritual darkness and light, between ordered society and anarchy. As Jesus said, "The thief comes only to kill, to steal and to destroy. I have come that human beings may have life, life in all its fullness" (John 10:10).

There is no life, however, without light. As we celebrate the birth of Jesus, we need to rescue his story from any romantic or legendary reading. The tiny light of life that flickered in the baby of Bethlehem was assailed by shadows of darkness and real danger that are similar to those confronting us today.

The religious fundamentalism that could justify stoning to death a young girl with a baby outside marriage was something that Jesus himself would challenge in the course of his ministry. The heavy hand of Roman dictatorship oppressed people under occupation, by moving them like pawns on the board: in this case compelling a young mother in the late stages of pregnancy to make an arduous journey from her home to elsewhere for administrative reasons to do with a poll tax. The poverty of their wider family is summed up in the Greek word *kataluma*, which we translate as "inn" but which probably signified a single-roomed dwelling with an upper platform for eating and sleeping with a lower part for the animals. If people were sleeping cheek by jowl on the platform, where else could a tiny baby be put safely but in a manger, in the sheltered corner set aside for small animals?

The early childhood of Jesus was upheaved by the atrocity of Herod, the local ruler set up by the Romans, whose ruthless character is recorded by the Jewish historian Josephus. Imitating the genocidal actions of Pharaoh long before him, his wholescale massacre of male children under the age of two in and around Bethlehem prompted the flight of Mary and Joseph and their child as refugees into Egypt. Christmas is still overshadowed by the tragic fact that there are more than 60 million displaced people in the world today, more than the whole population of the UK. In their faces, we see the pain of exile, mindful of the long-term consequences for their psychological happiness and wellbeing, and especially that of their children. Their heartbreak is ours too, and their vulnerability is now made worse by exposure to a pandemic in unhealthy surroundings.

Where, then, is God in the midst of such woe? It was Archbishop Michael Ramsey who once said that "Just when the problem of evil oppresses us, we are confronted with the challenge of goodness." In recent years we have seen terrorists and criminals behave in wicked and cruel ways; but at the same time we have seen human beings respond with courage and generous compassion. Which is the truly human behaviour? For there can be no neutral stance in the face of such a challenge. We need to be clear-headed about the chilling fact that evil always seeks to pull down human beings, to destroy their relationships, societies and cultures. The coming of Jesus into the world was, and is, the way in which God seeks our collaboration in confronting this darkness and overcoming it with his abundant life. For as our text from John's Gospel asserts, evil can neither master, understand nor quench the light of God's love revealed in the death and resurrection of Jesus Christ. There is thus a spiritual dimension to the evil that we all face.

The light of the Christmas story, however, enhances our vision of certain human traits that are very close to our own celebrations as families today: the fragility and wonder of a human baby; the courage and compassion of Mary and Joseph; the loyalty of their wider families in Nazareth and Bethlehem, without which this pregnancy could never have been safe-guarded. As we think again about Jesus as a tiny child, and call to memory our own children, that feeling of love and care, of tenderness and devotion strengthens not only our own family life, but also draws us closer to God himself. For he came into the world in the person of Jesus to draw us into his friendship and to communicate in human terms his love for us as human beings. Mary and Joseph were young people, by our standards probably older teenagers: yet their faith, courage and compassion enabled them to respond to the call of God, with all its risks, and to impart to Jesus that confidence with which he could address God intimately as "Abba"—"Father", which we also do every time we say the Lord's Prayer. So for Christians, the interests of children and young people must always be central to the Church's life and ethics, and to our compassion, example and generosity as well.

The most mysterious title for Jesus is the Old Testament word *Emmanuel*—"God-with-us". What does this mean? First, it means that what God and human beings have in common is greater than anything else, for we are made in his image and likeness. God comes to us in Jesus as our Maker and our Friend. It means also that we may discern the presence of Christ among us in the people whom we meet, whom we love and serve. As he himself said, "Inasmuch as you care for the least of my brethren you are caring for me" (Matthew 25:40). Christ also comes alongside us in times of difficulty and suffering, supremely in his empathy and compassion as "the human face of God". We may also discover, as Dietrich Bonhoeffer did in prison under the Nazis in 1944, that as Christians we are called "to stand by God in his hour of grieving". For the secret of Christianity is the deep and hidden reality of Christ at the heart of our lives, the wellspring of our courage and compassion. This we seek day by day in our prayers, as we read the Gospels, and as we come to Holy Communion: in the words of St Paul, "Christ within you: the hope of glory" (Colossians 1:27).

It is one thing, however, to believe that this darkness can never overcome divine light, but it is another thing to confront its terrible reality, as many of our fellow Christians are doing today. They, and we, need to know where we stand, from where we may draw the strength to withstand all that would obliterate life, love and liberty. If we make Christ the foundation of our lives and of our prayers, of our compassion and our giving, then we will discover the truth expressed in these words of Paul, springing from his own experience:

> I am convinced that there is nothing in death nor life, in the realm of spirits or evil powers, in the world as it now is, or in the world as it will be, in any of the forces of the universe in their height or depth—nothing in all creation that can separate us from the love of God in Jesus Christ our Lord.
>
> *Romans 8:38–9*

These words, used by King George VI at a dark moment in the Second Word War, point the way: "I said to the man at the gate of the year: 'Give me a light that I may tread safely into the unknown.' And he replied: 'Go out into the darkness and put your hand into the hand of God. That shall be to you better than any light, and safer than a known way.'" May this be your experience, and that of your families and friends this Christmas.

PART 2

Christmas and Epiphany

7

Christmas

No-one has seen God at any time: God the only-begotten, the
Son who is in the bosom of the Father, He has expressed Him.
John 1:18

How can the invisible God, the creator of the universe, express himself
in a tiny baby? What an extraordinary thought! Yet this is what we are
bidden to think about on Christmas Day. Let us be clear, first of all,
that we are not here to wallow in a religious fairy story; nor is there
anything sentimental about a baby being born in a stable full of animals.
The circumstances surrounding the birth of Jesus were gritty and hard,
very typical, alas, of the conditions in which too many people lived then,
as they still do across the world today. When Francis of Assisi invented
and popularized the Christmas crib, it was to bring home to ordinary
peasants in Italy the fact that Jesus was born among folk just like them.

This young couple, Mary and Joseph, were compelled to travel across
the country when Mary was in the later stages of pregnancy, at the bidding
of the Roman occupying power for the purposes of taxation: they were
moved like pawns on a board, as were many others at that time. Without
the protection of their wider families in Nazareth and in Bethlehem,
however, Mary could easily have been stoned to death for having a child
outside marriage. Crammed into a poor home, where the animals slept
on the lower level while human beings slept cheek by jowl on a platform
above them, where else would you put a tiny baby so that it would not
be crushed but in a manger? When they left their home in Nazareth,
they assumed they would soon return, but in fact they were obliged to
flee as refugees to Egypt to escape the brutality of Herod, the local mafia
boss. Many people have to exist and try to raise families in very similar

conditions today. Yet it was into this dangerous and precarious world that God came in the form of this tiny baby.

Why would God choose to do this? Augustine once said that "proud man could only be saved by the humble God". We know how we respond to a baby or a tiny child: what warmth of love and tenderness spring from deep within us, even at two in the morning! If we have this capacity for love, which surely defines best what it means to be a human being, how does this relate to God? We often say as Christians that "God is love"; and when we say this, we mean something more than simply a remote and comfortable "sugar daddy", who will sort everything out in the end and, whatever we do, will always love us. This is a fallacious caricature. As Christians, we think of God's compassion, revealed in the story of Jesus, and also of his suffering love demonstrated on the cross. But what unites both these expressions of divine love is something deeper: it is the mystery of unrequited divine love. We all know what it feels like when someone does not respond to our love for them, and if we are "in love" with someone and this happens it is a terrible torment.

This is also God's torment revealed in Jesus, having created human beings to live in a beautiful world as his children, made in his image and likeness. Yet so many human beings ignore God completely and desecrate his world by treating each other with great brutality. We see plenty of evidence of this in our world today, and throughout human history. The coming of God in the person of the child Jesus challenges our heartlessness and arrogance. Meanwhile God actively and urgently seeks our love. He stooped to be born in the child Jesus in Bethlehem in order to enter our lives by the surest route, which is our natural love of children. Jesus placed children at the heart of the kingdom of God, and we should place their interests at the heart of our society too.

The coming of Jesus in the form of a child is actually the foundation of Christian ethics. Can we make our society truly child-centred? This is the great challenge for every generation, including our own. Despite the best efforts of social services, education and healthcare, too many children still languish in poverty in our own society. Across the world the situation is often far worse. Great strides have been made in terms of legislation to protect children, but far more needs to be done with great urgency. Christmas puts the spotlight on the child in our midst in this way, just as their presence enriches our family life and celebrations each year. There are still too many places where women can be stoned to death for religious reasons, and there are as many refugees as the entire population of the United Kingdom—the highest levels since the end of the Second World War.

The challenge of Christmas goes to the very heart of our lives, as individuals and as communities. Why do we ignore the love of God as it reaches out to us in Jesus Christ? Perhaps its demands challenge too many of our values and priorities. Augustine also said that "God has made us for himself, and our hearts are empty and restless until they find their rest in him." Consumerism cannot meet that deep human need and nor can anything else. It is striking how the demands of the pandemic have called forth great compassion for those most vulnerable, the sick and the elderly. It is heartening to see that the order in which people receive inoculation starts with those most at risk. Are our priorities now being corrected?

You can connect with the Christmas story just once a year, or you can make it the foundation for your life and the life of your family and our society. You would not drop a baby or abuse a child, so why drop God as he comes to you in this way? In Holy Communion we receive a tiny wafer, which brings to us the humble love of God poured out in the death of Jesus on the cross. You are not likely to drop that wafer either—so do not drop God. Do not let the call of God in the child Jesus pass you by: if you do, you will miss the most important thing in the world that can change your life and make you more truly God's child. For it is in Jesus, as a child, and throughout his life and death, that God has expressed himself: do not let his love for you go unrequited.

8

In the Beginning was the Word

The Prologue to St John's Gospel

"In the beginning was the Word, and the Word was with God, and the Word was God. The same was in the beginning with God."

With these remarkable words, the foundation of Christian theology was laid once for all. There is a clear echo of the beginning of Genesis where God spoke and it was done. That opening chapter introduces the sense that there is plurality within God the Creator, who made human beings in "our image and likeness". In later Jewish theology, the Wisdom of God became the expression of the creating purpose of God, and the Hebrew term for "Word" means something that is thought, expressed and accomplished by God's power. At around the time when Genesis was composed, Plato in his *Timaeus* taught something very similar about the divine *Logos* or Word. The Jewish theologian Philo took this term up to indicate how the Greek text of the Bible, the Septuagint, could cohere with the highest philosophy of the Greeks. Later Christian theologians followed his lead, basing their argument on the theology of this Gospel prologue (John 1:1–18).

> *All things were made through him, and without him there was not anything made. That which has been made was life in him; and the life was the light of humanity. The light shines in the darkness and the darkness neither understands nor quenches it.*

Note here that the Word has become a person, no longer just the organizing principle of creation. This is paralleled by Paul in his letter to the Colossians: "The Son is the image of the invisible God, the first born of all creation, for in him all things were created . . . all things have been created through him and for him, and in him all things hold together" (Colossians 1:15–16). This means that Christ constitutes the key to understanding everything about God and his purpose in creating the world. Christ's work of redemption and sanctification is thus the fulfilment of God's creative purpose. The life given to human beings has a moral and spiritual nature and purpose, which finds its expression and fulfilment in the Word, who constitutes the light by which people should live. There is no life apart from the light which is Christ. To turn away from him is to enter one's own shadow, and to move towards a fatal darkness of our own choosing and making. The tragedy within the Gospel begins to appear.

> *There came a man, sent from God, whose name was John. He came as a witness to bear witness to the light, that all might believe in him. He was not that light, but came to bear witness to that light.*

This Gospel prologue, like the Creeds, is anchored in history, in the coming of John the Baptist with which all four Gospels begin. In this Gospel, it is apparent that the earliest disciples of Jesus were at first followers of John. The prologue and the Gospel address carefully his historic role and significance. The Greek word for "witness" is *martyr*; in the background of the Gospels it is the tragic fate of the last of the prophets, whose ministry and fate foreshadowed that of Jesus himself. The role of John the Baptist is thus as important overtly as is that of Mary the Mother of the Lord in a more hidden way, as Jesus himself affirmed elsewhere in the Gospels.

> *The true light, which enlightens everyone, was coming into the world. He was in the world, and the world was made through him, but the world knew him not. He came unto his own people, but they who were his own received him not.*

In the opening chapter of Genesis, light is the first and governing principle of creation. The divine light now comes into the created world as a human person, he who as the Word has been in dialogue with human beings throughout their history, and more specifically in the revealed scripture and tradition of the Jews. The Word comes in a hidden way, eluding the darkness of evil and veiling his power in order to enable genuine belief and love to spring forth in the hearts and minds of those who encounter him. Some do respond in this way—hence the Gospels. But many others do not: and so the paradox of the rejection of the Messiah is introduced, the apparent tragedy to which each Gospel is in its own way a prologue.

> *But as many as received him to them he gave the power (and right and capacity) to become children of God, to them that believe on his Name; who were born not of blood, nor of the will of the flesh, nor of the will of man, but of God.*

Here is the heart of the Gospel, an epitome of all that this evangelist will unfold. It is also indirectly his commentary on how Jesus himself came into the world in the womb of the Virgin Mary. The word "receive" implies welcome, willingness, love and understanding. Human beings are intended to become "children of God" by an act of divine grace and remaking. Ancestry, choice and influence may play their part, but salvation and new life in Christ is the gift of God alone. There is a new creation underway as human beings are recalled by the Word to the love of God. Christ comes to restore the broken relationship between humanity and God.

> *The Word became flesh and dwelt among us, full of grace and truth; and we beheld his glory, the glory of the only-begotten from the Father.*

"The Word became flesh": in this unique conjunction of words the mystery of the incarnation and of the cross is intimated. Neither in Greek philosophy nor in Greek-speaking Judaism was it ever envisaged that the Word of God would become "flesh". Yet this principle of the Word-made-flesh became the fundamental principle of Christian belief, even if its meaning took some centuries to elucidate. The word "flesh" signifies mortality, suffering, finitude. How could the divine principle of creation confine itself in this way, and to what purpose? Implicit in this text is memory of the transfiguration of the Lord, described in the other Gospels, though not in this one, intimated in the words, "we saw his glory". The language here is drawn from the Old Testament, from the vision of Moses and the experience of the Exodus. The Word "pitches his tent" among his people and once again his "glory" is manifest, "full of grace and truth". In the transfiguration, as in the baptism of Jesus, the unique relationship of Jesus to God as his Father was revealed as that of the "only-begotten" one, the Son whose existence is therefore eternal.

> *John bore witness of him and declared, saying, "This is he of whom*
> *I said that he who comes after me takes rank before me, for he*
> *existed before me."*

These words are reiterated in the formal testimony of John the Baptist later in this opening chapter. John's role in this Gospel is clear and crucial, pointing the way to the one who was to come, and hinting at his divine origin. Implicit here is the hidden but seminal relationship between John and Jesus that rested on more than kinship, as the other Gospels indicate.

> *For of his fullness have we all received, and grace for grace. Whereas*
> *the Law was given through Moses, grace and truth have come*
> *through Jesus Christ. No-one has seen God at any time: God the*
> *only-begotten, the Son in the bosom of the Father, he has expressed*
> *Him.*

Here, as elsewhere, the evangelist introduces his own commentary on what is being said. The concept of "fullness" in Christ finds expression also in Paul's letter to the Ephesians. In Christ, God gives himself fully; and in the humanity of Jesus, the true image and likeness of God is fully revealed. This is the mystery of the incarnation, how the divine light and love of God could become focused and expressed uniquely in a human person, "full of grace and truth". Divine grace heals and divine truth reveals; thus the purpose of the Law is fulfilled in Christ, who is the living Law of God expressed in a human person, as the transfiguration stories in the other Gospels also make clear.

The last verse has a complicated textual history as it broke new ground in Jewish-Christian theology. It asserts the fundamental truth of Judaism that no one can see God and live. In words later taken up by Hilary of Poitiers, the hardest textual reading speaks of "God-only-begotten, the Son who is intimate with the Father, he has expressed him" (John 1:18). For later Christian theology, this signified the mystery of the Trinity and the co-equal nature of the Father and the Son, the *homoousios* (of one substance) of the Nicene Creed. For this evangelist, the rest of his Gospel will demonstrate how Jesus "expressed" or "declared" God, as the living and life-giving Word, in whom the glory of God was hidden until revealed supremely upon the cross.

9

The Impact of the Incarnation

In a more religious society, the week after Christmas would be another Holy Week, containing several major feasts, to be observed with due ceremony. Instead there is a danger that these feasts are completely forgotten unless one of them falls on a Sunday. Yet between them they intimate the impact of the incarnation of Christ, evident in the subsequent life of the Church.

On the day after Christmas, the death of the first known martyr is celebrated: *Stephen*, whose death is recounted in the seventh chapter of the Acts of the Apostles. The critical thing to note is that Stephen was faithful unto death inasmuch as he prayed for his persecutors, one of whom became the apostle Paul. It was in this Christ-like attitude that Stephen proved closest to his Lord, whom he saw in the glory of heaven just before he was killed by a stone-throwing mob. The pattern of his dying for his faith was repeated by many early Christian martyrs, whose commemoration became the foundation of the later cult of saints in Christianity. Martyrdom was already a feature of Judaism at the time of Stephen's death, and many Jews would die at Masada rather than surrender to the Romans after the fall of Jerusalem in AD 70. Sometimes the violent resistance fighters, called Zealots, would seek such an end. But in Christianity there is no record of any Christian martyr taking up weapons against their Roman or Jewish persecutors. To be a Christian martyr is to be a witness to the saving power of the death and resurrection of Jesus.

Two days after Christmas is the feast of the great evangelist, *John*. His Gospel is of overwhelming importance for Christian belief and theology, and its famous prologue is read as the climax of carol services and also on Christmas Day itself. It tells how "the Word became flesh . . . and we saw his glory" (John 1:14). The whole Gospel is a setting forth of this decisive witness. The miracles of Jesus reveal his divine identity just as his teaching communicates the truth of God revealed in him. The Fourth Gospel tells some wonderful human stories, such as the Samaritan woman who met Jesus at the well, or the way in which Mary Magdalene encountered the risen Jesus. The Gospel also contains crucial historical information which complements that in the three synoptic Gospels. It tells of the ministry of Jesus in and around Jerusalem, shedding light, for example, on the political context of the feeding of the five thousand: it was approaching Passover, which had become an annual protest against Roman rule, and the people wanted to turn Jesus into a Messianic king. The Gospel of John is therefore a key to understanding the other Gospels and their meaning.

On the third day after Christmas, we recall the grim context in which the birth of Jesus is recounted in Matthew's Gospel. After the departure of the Magi, the paranoid local ruler, Herod, decided to massacre all the male children in and around Bethlehem aged two years or younger, commemorated as the *Memorial of the Holy Innocents*. This indicates that when the Magi appeared on the scene, Jesus was already a young child rather than a baby. His family had to flee as refugees to Egypt to wait there until Herod was dead. Thus the shadow of the cross falls over the very beginning of Jesus' life. This event demonstrates once again the precarious plight of his parents as well as the barbarity of the age. Throughout Christian history, this story has served as a spotlight of reproach upon cruelty towards children in particular, and it is a shameful fact that such massacres continue today. The feast therefore serves to underpin Christian commitment to human rights and to the morality of proper child-care throughout the world.

The fourth feast after Christmas, observed in England, is not without controversy: it marks the murder of *Thomas Becket* in Canterbury Cathedral in 1170. Henry VIII tried completely to eradicate all memory of Becket after the Reformation, but in the Middle Ages across Europe, Becket was remembered as a martyr for the liberty and integrity of the Church, a potent symbol challenging arbitrary royal rule. He had been a friend of King Henry II, who assumed that by appointing him to be Archbishop of Canterbury, he would prove to be an ally. But Becket, once in post, saw himself as a trustee of the Church of Canterbury, as well as part of a wider controversy at the time in Western Europe about the role of the king in appointing bishops. Becket's faithfulness to his duty as archbishop and his personal courage in the face of intimidation secured his memory. I remember Archbishop Michael Ramsey telling me that it was only when he found himself in the hotseat at Canterbury that he came to understand and appreciate better the significance of Becket's stand. The point is that Christian leaders sometimes have to make a stand on principle for the sake of the Gospel, often in the midst of confusing and murky historical circumstances, and this continues, as Christians are the largest group of people facing persecution in many parts of the world today.

Each of these feasts, so often overlooked in the welter of consumerism and family life, reflect ways in which the coming of Christ has affected life and thought, the values of society and the duties of individual Christians throughout history up to the present time. The light of Christ continues to shine into the darkness of human affairs, and it has not been quenched.

1 0

Seraphim of Sarov

2 January

*Beloved, even now we are children of God; but it is not yet made
manifest what we shall be. We know, however, that if He shall be
manifested, we shall be like Him, for we shall see Him as He is.*

1 *John 3:2*

As a young priest, for many years I used to make my retreat at Fairacres
Convent in Oxford in the cell of St Seraphim of Sarov. As I went to and
fro to the offices, I would catch the eye of a small box-wood carving of
St Seraphim, and rather idly I wondered who he was. Then in later years,
friendship with Orthodox Christians drew him to my attention more
seriously and I first read the remarkable book *Flame in the Snow* by Julia
de Beausobre, who survived a Soviet concentration camp and fled to the
safety of England before the Second World War. Her writing drew on the
testimonies of people living near Sarov in central Russia during those
terrible years, whose memories went back to those who had known the
saint in the nineteenth century.

Seraphim died in 1834 and was canonized in 1903 in the presence of
the Tsar. But twenty years later his shrine was desecrated and his relics
carted off to a museum of atheism, where all trace of them was lost for
many long and bitter years. Why was the memory of this saint such a
threat to the Communist regime? What I did not realize at the time,
however, was that researching the history and spiritual significance of
this very recent saint would prepare the way for many valuable and
transforming meetings with Orthodox Christians in Russia and elsewhere
in the former Soviet empire as it was collapsing.

So it was that in 1991 I found myself celebrating a double Easter: first with Latvian Lutherans in Riga, where for the first time Easter banners decorated the streets; then the next weekend in Moscow with Orthodox friends, along with my wife, during which we kept Easter night with its long and beautiful services at the shrine of St Sergius, in his great monastery at what was then called Zagorsk. But before we made the snowy journey there from Moscow, we went straight from the station to a cathedral in which the newly recovered relics of Seraphim were being venerated. They had been discovered in the basement of the museum of atheism in Leningrad and restored to the Russian church amid great rejoicing. After Moscow, they were transferred that year to Diveyevo to become again a focus of pilgrimage and a place of healing in the convent which the saint had founded there.

This was the first Easter of freedom: long trestles were heavily laden with Russian Easter cakes to be openly blessed and censed by the priests. We joined the long queue that snaked into and through the church, waiting our turn to kneel briefly before the gilt casket with its glass lid in which the relics of Seraphim lay under velvet covers, with just a small circle cut away to reveal the skull. As we moved away, there was a stir: word had got out that pilgrims from England had come to venerate the saint, and to our amazement and some embarrassment we were led back to the casket, where the lid was thrown open for us to venerate the relics and spend longer in their presence. It was a most moving honour and a characteristic act of Orthodox graciousness, and for us all it was a moment of unique encounter with the living presence of so loving a saint.

Thereafter, as Russia lurched from crisis to crisis in its emergence from Communism, and as the Orthodox Church there adapted and reacted to changing circumstances, Seraphim was rarely absent for long from our thoughts and prayers. His presence and influence was everywhere we went: in the wooden church of the *Poustinka*—a convent deep in the forests of Jelgava in Latvia; at the ancient Pechersk Lavra in Kiev, where relics associated with him were still treasured, and where he received his vocation to become a monk confirmed by a *staretz* who, unknown to him and others at the time, was in fact a holy woman. Meanwhile, as contacts between churches opened up, Seraphim emerged as one of the most accessible and loveable of Russian saints—a saint for the whole

Church alongside Francis of Assisi. So it is that his feast, the day of his death in 1834, is commemorated today in the Anglican calendar.

So who was Seraphim and why is he so important? Fortunately the sources of information for his life are sound and plentiful and have been recently edited in an excellent English translation. He was born in the middle of the eighteenth century and grew up in a Christian home. It was with the encouragement of his mother that he pursued the monastic life at the monastery of Sarov in central Russia in 1778–9. After some years as a monk, he sought permission in 1794 to retreat into the deep forest as a hermit. He turned the environment around his cell into a replica of the Holy Land and read the Gospel each day. He paid particular devotion to the memory of our Lady and used the Jesus Prayer as the core of his prayer and meditation.

The heart of his spirituality is captured in these words:

> If you would order the inner dwelling-place of your soul, first of all prepare the necessary material so that the heavenly architect can begin the building. The house must be light and airy, with windows, which are the five senses, so that the light of heaven, the sun of righteousness, can penetrate to our inner dwelling. The door of the house is Christ in person, for he said, "I am the door". He guards the house and lives in it. Yes, if your soul is prepared, God can come in and dwell there.

But it was not all sweetness and light. His was a hard and afflicted path; he was sought out by many unhappy and confused people and subject to jealousy from his fellow monks. He withdrew further from human contact for a long while, praying night and day upon a stone and feeding himself with the fruits of the forest. This continued until he narrowly escaped death at the hands of some criminals, who left him disabled. He steeped himself in the hesychast tradition of Orthodox prayer rooted in Mount Athos and withdrew into utter silence. But in 1810 he was summoned back to the monastery at Sarov, where he enclosed himself in his cell for five years. Then in 1815 he emerged to begin a remarkable ministry of spiritual direction and healing as a *staretz* or elder. His message was simple: "Learn to be peaceful and thousands around you will find salvation." He loved animals and also children, greeting his many visitors with the words "My joy!" As a child, who once met him, observed, "You know, Father Seraphim only looks like an old man, but he's really a child like us."

Throughout his monastic life Seraphim had a particular affinity with women and was much sought after as a spiritual director; sometimes this caused him difficulties and his visitors had to be curtailed. His most remarkable and abiding achievement was the nurturing of a convent nearby at Diveyevo, which comprised a small group of nuns whom he directed but seldom met. This was supported by a close circle of his friends from whom many of the most important memories about him arose. In 1825, Seraphim felt called by the Holy Mother of God herself to develop a new dimension of the convent's life: the creation of a mill where a group of younger nuns might live. The place where this vocation occurred was marked by a holy spring of water. By 1829, a church had been built as well. Seraphim regarded St Mary as the abbess of this new community and marked it out with a moat as a spiritual as well as a physical rampart. Despite the jealousy of the local bishop, this community at the mill was to symbolize the glorious transfiguration of the world through love.

The spiritual significance of Seraphim was and is profound. It lay behind the Optina hermitage, which exercised such a great spiritual influence on Russian Christian life before the revolution and beyond. His memory gave hope through the dark years of Communist persecution, which he predicted. Seraphim's life demonstrated the renewal of human nature that is possible in this life by the indwelling of the Holy Spirit, and through a lifetime's sharing in the suffering of Christ in compassion for others, through conflict with evil, which was also intercession for the world. His was a truly transfigured and transfiguring life that could kindle in the hearts of those who met him the fire of God's redeeming and healing love. It was his own insistence on the reality of the Holy Spirit and the nearness of the resurrection that marked out his spiritual charisma and prophetic authority.

His neighbour heard him singing the Easter hymns in his cell the day before he died, kneeling before his beloved icon of the Mother of God of Tenderness. He became a truly Christ-like person in whom the reality and meaning of baptism, the Eucharist and the priesthood became embodied. So today we echo the words of the Orthodox liturgy for his feast: "Rejoice, O blessed Seraphim, with the joy of the Kingdom, which you have already tasted on earth!"

1 1

Epiphany

Light, life and love

Epiphany is a much older feast than Christmas, and it revolves around three events in the Gospels: the Wise Men following the star to Bethlehem; the Baptism of Jesus by John the Baptist in the River Jordan; and the first miracle of Jesus at Cana in Galilee, as recorded in John's Gospel, where Jesus turned water into wine and so began to reveal his divine glory.

The word "Epiphany" means the shining forth of light upon someone, as in the words of Paul: "God who commanded the light to shine out of darkness has shone in our hearts to give the light of the knowledge of the glory of God in the face of Jesus Christ" (2 Corinthians 4:6). In Christ, the invisible light of God became incarnate and expressed in a human person, focused through Jesus as through a lens. All through the Gospels, in various ways, the light of God's presence in Jesus peeps out in all he taught and did, coming to a hidden focal point in the transfiguration and also on the cross. His light illumines, but it also exposes; it heals, but it also judges those who prefer the darkness because their deeds are evil. To turn to the light of Christ is to live in that light; but to turn away is to enter the shadow of sin, with fatal and evil consequences.

In the light of Christ, the life of God became manifest. Jesus said that he had come to give life in all its fullness, and this certainly accounts for the pattern of his teaching and activities. In many ways, the account of the baptism of Jesus mirrors that of the creation of the world in Genesis 1. The Spirit hovered over the waters of creation as the Spirit hovered over the person of Christ as he was baptized. The voice of God the Father and Creator was also active in both narratives, for in Christ a new creation was revealed. His coming into human history is to restore fullness of life to human beings, and to enable them to return to God, who is their loving heavenly Father. The life of God in Christ plunges into the depths of all the disorder in human nature and in creation to make all things new. The baptism of Jesus thus anticipates his death on the cross, where evil tried to overcome and destroy the light and life of God himself in its relentless assault on humanity made in God's image and likeness.

How is evil overcome and how is human nature renewed? Here the miracle of transformation of water into wine gives a clue. It takes place at a wedding, in the context of human life and love. It occurs as a response to the loving but urgent request of Mary, the mother of Jesus. It reveals the generosity of divine love as it overflows into human life, because the best wine is produced last, reversing common human practice. In the Bible, marriage between a man and a woman is one of the most potent symbols of the relationship between God and his people, and also between Christ and the Church, which includes each human soul that is in union with him. Jesus is referred to in the Gospels as the bridegroom seeking his bride. The crucial and painful question of the Gospels is whether his love will be welcomed and accepted, or whether it will be rejected. Part of the tragedy of the cross lies in the unrequited love of God for human beings, who are his children and made in his image and likeness, for divine love can never force its way into a human heart.

Light—Life—Love: these three words encapsulate the message of Epiphany, providing an important key to reading the Gospels as an epiphany that is manifest in the teaching and activities of Jesus. They also help to account for the final collision on the cross between the love of God and the evil destruction of human nature, trapped in un-love and sin. The transfiguration and the resurrection appearances are equally steeped in this threefold pattern of light and life and love. Why is this so?

Epiphany is the feast that lays the foundation of what is distinctive about Christian belief about the nature of God: that God is Trinity— Father, Son and Holy Spirit—and this is revealed in the story of the baptism of Jesus. Light gives and sustains Life; and the character of divine Light and Life is Love, for "God is love". From the Father springs the light of creation; in the incarnate Son is embodied the life-giving life of God that renews all things; in the Spirit is mediated divine love to unite the whole divine work of creation, redemption and sanctification. But light, life and love are true of every person of God as well, Father, Son and Holy Spirit. This is the mystery and the abyss of God's love to which human beings are called and into which Christians are committed by their own baptism. The holy triangle of light and life and love are manifested also in the sacrament of Holy Communion, which is participation in each and all of these divine realities: "Receive the Body of Christ; taste of the fountain of life: for with Thee, O Lord, is the well of life; and in thy light shall we see light."

On 9 November 1906, a young woman died of a terrible disease in Dijon in France: she was only twenty-six years old, and her name was Sister Elizabeth of the Trinity, a Carmelite nun, who has since been beatified by Pope John Paul II in 1984 and more recently canonized. Her message to her younger married sister summed up her own intimate relationship with God in Christ: "He is the one who never changes. He loves you today as he loved you yesterday; and as he will love you tomorrow." Her very last words, uttered as she was dying, were these: "I am going to light, to love and to life." How wonderful that one so young, in the midst of such suffering, could experience and articulate the heart of the mystery of the Epiphany, which is the key to the meaning of the whole purpose of God revealed in Jesus Christ, and made present and real by the indwelling of the Holy Spirit.

Antony of Egypt

17 January

To visit the great monastery of St Antony, which is not far from the Red Sea in Egypt, is to go to the heart of Coptic Christianity. Many of its buildings and chapels are very old and it is enclosed by a great wall. In the old days, visitors were hoisted up in a basket for reasons of security. None of the present buildings date back to the time of Antony, however, who died in the middle of the fourth century at the grand old age of 105. But his cave remains in the mountainside above the monastery as a holy place of pilgrimage and prayer.

There are three principal sources for the life of Antony, and by far the most important is the *Life* written by St Athanasius, who knew him personally and to whom Antony left his cloak after his death. This *Life* spread far and wide throughout the Christian world in the fourth century and thereafter. It was instrumental in the conversion of Augustine, and the memory of Antony spread as far as England, where his famous meeting with Paul the hermit is portrayed on the Ruthwell Cross and on other Anglo-Saxon carvings.

Antony was born around the year 251 and died in 356, so his life straddled the transition in the life of the Church from persecution to establishment under Constantine and his successors. Antony himself intervened in some of the later persecutions and also on the side of Athanasius in the Arian controversy in Alexandria. As a teenager and orphan, prompted by the Lord's command to the rich young man in the Gospel to sell everything in order to become perfect, Antony sold his family property, placed his younger sister in a community of holy women, and became a local hermit. In due time, he was led into the desert where for many years he continued a life of solitary prayer and spiritual conflict. Others came to follow his example and the last part of his life was spent as a spiritual father and teacher. The *Life* by Athanasius recounts his spiritual odyssey, incorporating a lengthy homily by Antony himself on the nature of the monastic life. The way that Athanasius set about his task constituted a model for much later monastic hagiography.

The *Life* by Athanasius is corroborated by numerous sayings from the Desert Fathers about Antony along with several letters that he wrote to various people. This means that a clear picture of the saint's character and teaching can be pieced together in many memorable episodes. His own life and example embodied what he believed to be the true way of following Jesus, demonstrating firstly the reality of individual choice in a society which denied choice to so many people. Secondly it demonstrated the meaning of spiritual struggle or *ascesis*, which is lifelong and arduous, in response to the command of the Lord to Antony to "pay attention to yourself". Thirdly, Antony experienced severe spiritual conflict with evil, within his personal spiritual life and also coming from other people: this is graphically described and analysed in the *Life* by Athanasius. Spiritual conflict was closely related to relentless temptations, and Antony's view was that there is no way into the kingdom of God without encountering temptation, which exercises a person's moral choice for God at every turn. Finally, the duty of diligent prayer was laid upon all: Antony said, "I will have no mercy on you, nor will God have any either, if you yourself do not make an effort and if you do not pray to God."

When Antony emerged from long seclusion, Athanasius portrayed him as Adam restored, in fine physical form and at peace with the beauty of his environment. There was no inner dualism, no conflict between body and spirit, and this was an important witness in a society bowed down by chronic suffering and frequent deaths. For them, unlike ourselves, the body could too easily be felt to be the prison of the soul. Antony's witness was to the reality of the resurrection and to Christ's work of grace in restoring a person in the image and likeness of God, as he did in the Gospels. As a result, Antony's life became a life-giving role model for others, a sign of the reality and compassion of God.

> In the midst of a severe conflict with evil, light suddenly appeared
> from heaven which drove his adversaries away. As Antony caught
> his breath, he asked the Lord, "Where were you? Why did you not
> appear at the beginning to make my suffering cease?" The reply
> came, "Antony, I was here, but I waited to watch your fight. Since
> you have endured and not been overcome, I will always help you
> and make your name known far and wide."

The outward sign of this victory was Antony's frequent making the sign
of the cross by which evil was repelled. This testimony speaks directly
to so many of us, isolated at home and oppressed by anxiety about the
course and impact of the pandemic.

The sayings of Antony are similarly robust and to the point:

> Our life and our death is with our neighbour. If we gain our
> brother or sister, we have gained God. But if we scandalize our
> brother or sister, we have sinned against Christ.

There are many stories told about his wisdom and compassion as a pastor
of souls; and there was a stability to his life which he commended to
others:

> Just as fish die if they stay too long out of water, so monks or
> nuns who loiter outside their cells and pass their time gossiping
> with men or women of the world lose their inner peace. So like
> fish going towards the sea, we must hurry to reach our cell, for
> fear that if we delay outside we will lose our inner watchfulness.

Can we make this spirit of "inner watchfulness" our own during this
current period of enforced seclusion? An old monk once asked God
to grant him a vision of the holy fathers in heaven, but he noticed that
Antony was absent. So he asked, "Where is Abba Antony?" He was told
in reply that in the place where God is, there Antony would be:

> Three fathers used to go and visit blessed Antony every year, and
> two of them used to discuss their thoughts and the salvation of

their souls with him, but the third always remained silent and did not ask him anything. After a long time, Abba Antony said to him, "You often come here to see me, but you never ask me anything". The other replied, "It is enough for me to see you, Father."

The secret of Antony's life and its impact on others lay in these words for which he was long remembered: "I no longer fear God, but I love him: for love casts out fear." It is the duty of Christians at the present time to drive away fear by their example and by their fervent prayers. For Antony also said that "the vision of the holy ones is not fraught with distraction. It comes so quietly and gently that immediately joy, gladness and courage arise in the soul. For the Lord, who is our joy, is with them." Let us pray that Christ may be with us, and with all those whom we love, near and far, and bring us all his peace as he has promised to do by saying, "I am with you always."

1 3

The Conversion of Paul

25 January

Paul is unique among the writers of the New Testament for the autobiographical testimony at the heart of his letters. The account of his dramatic conversion is recounted three times in the Acts of the Apostles. However people react to him, there can be no doubt that the inner spiritual conflicts within Paul's personality and experience are everywhere apparent. His conversion, which began so dramatically on the road to Damascus, proved to be a continuous process, and often a painful one, throughout the whole of his life. As a result, much light is shed on what it meant for a Jewish Pharisee to become a Christian, as many of them evidently did. The severe conflict within Judaism induced by the preaching of Christ almost tore Paul apart. The inclusion of Gentiles within Christianity, though not within all of the Jewish Law, posed to early Jewish Christianity its first most potent threat and challenge. Paul's life was a crucible in which the early Church was formed and its essential nature articulated.

At the same time, Paul is the first among Christian saints to express directly what it felt like to be "in Christ", as he describes it so often. His own mission and ministry were literally driven by the Holy Spirit, often along hazardous and lonely paths. In his dialogue with other early Christian leaders, he frequently found himself at loggerheads because of his loyalty to the vision of Christ as he had received it. Yet subsequent Christianity has affirmed the stand that he took; otherwise his letters would never have been so carefully collected and preserved, or regarded as authoritative and apostolic in nature.

In the West, his significance as a fount of systematic doctrine at the hands of Augustine, and later still of Luther, has perhaps eclipsed his abiding role as the foremost spiritual father in the long tradition of Christian ascetic life and prayer. Yet frequently the language of Christian sanctity and spiritual testimony, Eastern and Western, echoes with the words of Paul. The most striking early example of this within the tradition of the British Church is to be found in the *Confession* of St Patrick, written in the early fifth century. The fusion of mission, suffering and vision is the same.

The content of the vision which Paul sought and encountered in Christ may be discerned in his writings as he tried to describe the indescribable "glory of God in the face of Jesus Christ", and to explore its implications for Christian life and belief. Paul is therefore a mystic, a person whose whole life has been drawn to the threshold of eternity and is being transformed as a result. The mystical aspect of Paul's testimony is one of the reasons for his subsequent authority as a spiritual father. The essentially Jewish character of his mystical experience and its expression has been elucidated in a number of major studies of first-century Jewish apocalyptic mysticism—a visionary tradition of great eloquence that looked to the end of the age and beyond. Paul emerges as a prime witness to the vitality, depth and nature of this powerful tradition within Judaism.

At the same time, this tradition sheds invaluable light upon Paul's testimony, and indeed upon the whole New Testament vision of Christ. As the writer of the letter to Hebrews asserted: "the blood of Jesus makes us free to enter the sanctuary with confidence by the new and living way which Christ has opened for us . . . the way of his flesh" (Hebrews 10:19–20). What is unique about the visionary way in the New Testament is that it is the way of the cross: the glory of God is discovered within and through the sufferings of Christ.

In the two principal autobiographical passages of Paul's writings, in Philippians 3 and in 2 Corinthians, he set forth the nature of this way of living through dying. Therein lies his unique authority as a spiritual guide. His insistence upon this way directly colours his whole theology as a Christian. All the main lines of his teaching—justification by faith; the indwelling of the Holy Spirit; the Church as the Body of Christ; the tragedy of Israel's partial refusal of Jesus as the Messiah; his eschatological vision; and his ethical teaching—all are marked by the central experience of Crucifixion–resurrection at the heart of Christian life as he knew it.

Paul's mysticism was genuinely apocalyptic in the sense that his vision was set upon "the glory of God revealed in the face of Jesus Christ", something to be sought after and apprehended as the true and present goal of earthly life. But the cost of this vision was ever deeper suffering, as Christ became formed in him through the spiritual conflict that he encountered within and around him. This was his witness, his living martyrdom, finally sealed by his death in Rome. What was the experience of the resurrection life, however, as his mission unfolded? How did he discern this in the light of his vision of Christ crucified? What is the bearing of this vision for the life of the Church today?

These words of Archbishop Michael Ramsey in his first book, *The Gospel and the Catholic Church*, sum up the experience of St Paul, and of so many saints, known and unknown, who have found themselves "in Christ". "Not only did crucifixion make possible the giving of the Holy Spirit, but the life bestowed by the Spirit is a life of which crucifixion is a quality, a life of living through dying." Perhaps the key to penetrating the inner experience of resurrection is to be found in Paul's language of prayer, which occurs throughout his letters. For he believed that it is the prayer of the Spirit of Christ within a person that transforms their life as they become drawn within the living beam of God's love. To kneel at the *confessio* where Paul is buried under the high altar of the lovely basilica of St Paul Outside the Walls in Rome, is to draw very near to the apostle to the Gentiles.

1 4

Candlemas

This lovely feast marks the end of Christmas. Its various titles—The Purification of the Blessed Virgin Mary; The Presentation of Christ in the Temple; The Meeting of Christ with his holy people—signify the rich panoply of meanings to be considered. The story comes among the private family memories which Luke included at the beginning of his Gospel and whose authority was largely that of Mary, the Mother of Jesus, herself.

First, it reminds us that human life was precious and precarious in those days as indeed it is in ours. After forty days both child and mother could be regarded as safe from immediate death in or around childbirth. The idea of purification may seem anachronistic today, perhaps, but the service of the Churching of Women in the *Book of Common Prayer* signifies that this dimension of relief and thanksgiving for the safe delivery of a child was considered of real value not so long ago.

In the Jewish tradition, the Law prescribed the offering of all first-born animals and human beings to God. In the case of a male child, it recalled also the birth of Isaac, the child of promise to elderly parents, through whom Jews claimed their descent from Abraham and their share in the covenant of God. Behind this lies the ancient and fundamental principle of the Bible that the first and the best should always be offered to God. This too finds its place in our own ancient tradition at Lammastide, when until relatively recently the first bread was baked from the first sheaves of wheat and offered at the beginning of August as a thank-offering for harvest. Harvest festivals are a modern creation of the later nineteenth century. This offering of the first and the best mirrors God's own offering of himself in his Son, Jesus Christ: "for God so loved the world that He gave His only Son" (John 3:16).

The presentation of Jesus in the Temple represented the coming of God's Messiah, as promised in the Old Testament, into the heart of the religion of Israel. Into this splendid Temple building, recently renovated by Herod the Great and famous throughout the ancient world for its beauty, this young couple now brought their first tiny child. Christ came to fulfil and to transfigure the faith of his people, to be the glory of Israel. His light and love illuminate every aspect of all that was of value in that religion. But if the Temple is like an elaborate lantern filled with the light of Christ, its shutters were to now be flung open so that the light and love of God could shine across the world, attracting all peoples—the Gentiles—to himself. This is the double destiny of the Christ-child, "for God so loved the world".

Christ's mission would not be welcome to all, however, as the old man Simeon intimated to the parents of Jesus: in fact it would cause scandal and division, ending in tragedy. Simeon and Anna represent the faithful vocation of all the laity in the life of Israel and also in the subsequent life of the Church. Their diligence in their worship and prayers laid the foundation for their spiritual awareness and pastoral sensitivity, as this story demonstrates. It reminds us how essential it is that all are welcomed when they come into church, and especially the young as they come for baptism, confirmation and marriage. Such loving encounters can change lives and feed the memory, drawing people closer to the love of God. It is essential that children and young people in particular sense the consistent welcome and kindness of the church as a place where they can feel secure and valued in their own right.

I remember a striking example of this kind of pastoral encounter when we were visiting Cologne. We were in one of the lovely Romanesque churches there that had been restored after being bombed by our air force during the last war. It was dedicated to St Alban and had some of his relics in an elaborate enamel casket made in the twelfth century in Limoges in France. Suddenly a little old lady in a blue deacon's robe emerged, clutching a large ewer of water for a baptism. I always remember her when I hear about Anna in this Gospel. I spoke to her in German, and she made us very welcome in the church. Then she asked me where we came from in Germany. I demurred, so she asked if we were Danish. I said that I was English. "Ah! So you have come at last." She had seen all the horrors that we had inflicted on her city though she did not mention them. In conversation with the young priest there, he showed how the beautiful reliquary of Limoges enamel of St Alban had been carefully restored after bomb damage. Some of the new enamel panels now portrayed the RAF planes over their city. It was a sombre encounter in the middle of a very sad visit to Cologne. Yet it was from that church that a relic of St Alban was given to the abbey church in England that bears his name.

So Candlemas is overshadowed by the cross, by the sombre words of Simeon to Mary that what would happen to her son would break her heart. Only Mary could have remembered such terrible words, which haunted her life as she supported Jesus in his ministry, fending off family pressure, and fielding unkind insinuations about the circumstances of his birth, then following him to Jerusalem to witness his betrayal, torture and death on the cross. A horrific prospect for any parent—but one experienced all too often in many parts of the world today. Mary's was true martyrdom as the Mother of the Lord.

Thus we come full circle to the beginning—to the offering of the first and the best to God. The self-offering of Christ for the redemption of humanity was completed on the cross. It reveals that sacrifice lies at the heart of God's love and that his self-giving in Christ is at great cost, and can only be received at great cost, as the Mother of Jesus experienced. "Behold, I am the servant of the Lord; may it be to me according to your word" (Luke 1:38). Abraham was as right as he was wrong when he felt impelled to offer Isaac, his child of promise, to God in thanksgiving and sacrifice (Genesis 22). His action mirrored that of God himself, who instead provided the sacrifice that would spare the life of Isaac, and in Christ of all humanity. "For God so loved the world, that He gave His only begotten Son, that whoever believes in him should not perish but should have eternal life" (John 3:16).

Seeking the Kingdom of God

*"Seek first the kingdom of God and His righteousness
and everything else will be added to you."*

These words of Jesus (Matthew 6:33) pose a direct challenge to every generation of human society. They were a challenge to the mostly poor folk who first heard his message, and whose lives were ruled by chronic anxiety bred from poverty. They are a challenge today to a society hooked on consumer capitalism, but that now faces unravelling because of its inroads into the environment, the gross inequalities it has created across the world and the impact of a pandemic. So how can we seek again the kingdom of God and its values?

The Ten Commandments (Exodus 20:1–17) are a good place to begin. Note that they are commandments to be obeyed, not just an advisory to be considered. They pose the sharp question: "What do you really want in your life, and what, or whom, do you value most?" They invite our choice, and they correct our values. If you approach them from the last commandment first, the rest follow quite logically. To covet something is to value it in the wrong way; to envy someone is to see them as an enemy. The Genesis story of Adam and Eve, followed by that of Cain and Abel, epitomizes the impact of breaking these divine commandments. Eve coveted something forbidden her and lured her husband into complicity with her crime. She stole from God; and much of the way the natural environment is plundered today is in the same spirit. Her choice disrupted her sexual relationship with her husband because unfaithfulness had been allowed to intrude. This is the root and wider meaning of adultery, the disruption of family relationships by cruelty, abuse, neglect, or by immorality in misusing sexuality.

Cain envied his brother and resented him, and this actually became apparent to him in the context of his worship of God. He ignored his conscience, however, lured his brother into the wilderness, and stole his life by murdering him, thus showing complete contempt for their parents. All the commandments governing human relationships were thus broken in the beginning of Genesis, and this chronic pattern of destructive behaviour can be detected throughout human history, and certainly throughout the Bible. Christ himself was a victim of such behaviour, a victim of betrayal and cruelty; and of course he challenged human sin by his own teaching and example.

The first four commandments provide the foundation for overcoming these wrong choices and values. If people truly believe in God, they will quickly realize that they are accountable to him, both for the gift of life itself and also for how they should behave. Atheism and ignoring God undermines in the end the moral cohesion of individuals, families and society. Hiding in the bushes, as it were, and clutching fig leaves is folly and delusion, as a person cannot hide from God, as the opening Collect for Purity makes clear in the Eucharist—"cleanse the thoughts of our hearts". Yet it was this dishonesty that has consistently corrupted the relationship between God and human beings from the beginning; Christ came into the world to restore trust between God and his children.

The second commandment warns against valuing the creation more than its Creator, or elevating a person into some kind of cult figure to be worshipped. This is the meaning of idolatry, and its modern forms in terms of dictatorship and media cults of personality are no less bewitching and dangerous for all involved. The third commandment reminds us that belief in God consists of a relationship with him, not just a distant belief about him. For Christians, the Name of God has taken human form in the person of Christ, who is the focus of our loyalty and love. The fourth commandment speaks about the right ordering of time, primarily for the worship of God, but also to safeguard human life from all forms of slavery, imposed or voluntary. This challenges the modern seven-day cycle of restless activity, shopping, news and sport that has destroyed the keeping of Sunday in our country and undermined the life of the Church.

The hinge between the two parts of the Ten Commandments affirms respect for parents as the proper foundation of all social morality. We know how much sorrow, mischief and crime is caused by poor parenting. All of us—parents, godparents, grandparents, teachers and clergy—have an absolute duty consistently to mirror to children the love of God as their true Father. Implicit in this commandment, therefore, is the respect that parents should show to their children and their friends. The foundation of all morality is example based upon trust, and breaking any of the other commandments breaches this trust between people in various and interlocked ways.

Christ confirmed the fundamental importance of these commandments when he said that people must love God with all their heart, mind, soul and strength, and love their neighbours as themselves. To this he added further teaching about what this love of others should mean. He taught that those who follow him must love others as he has loved them: his own example of compassion, self-sacrifice and self-giving, is of paramount importance here. He also carried out his own injunction to love enemies and persecutors as he was being nailed to the cross. This love of enemies and commitment to reconciliation based upon true forgiveness is the ultimate test of Christianity, its distinctive hallmark and permanent challenge to us all. Only by obedience to the teaching and example of Jesus can we actually seek first the kingdom of God and his righteousness. So his question to us remains: "What do you really want, and what, and whom, do you most value?" For if Christ is not lord of all our life, he cannot be Lord at all.

1 6

The Temptations of Jesus

For hundreds of years, Lent has always begun with consideration of the temptations of Jesus as recorded in the Gospels of Matthew and Luke (Matthew 4; Luke 4). Lent itself is modelled in part on the forty days that Jesus spent in the desert after his baptism. But the temptations of Jesus were not confined to this period of his life, and the letter to Hebrews recalls how "he was tempted like us in all things, but without sin" (Hebrews 4:15). In the Gospels, the pressure on Jesus could be enormous, even from his closest friends—"get behind me, Satan!" were stern words for Peter when he tried to dissuade Jesus from going to Jerusalem to suffer and die. In the garden of Gethsemane, and also on the cross, Jesus was sorely tempted: "if you are the Son of God, come down from the cross!" The story of the temptations in the desert provides a powerful clue to the pressures that were upon him throughout his ministry. What sort of Messiah was he going to be?

The temptations of Jesus reveal the expectations of the Jewish people at that time for a Messiah who would deliver them from oppression: from the ravages of poverty, the brutality of Roman occupation, and the corruption of senior clergy at the Temple in Jerusalem. All this is well documented from other historical sources. Jesus came perilously close to fulfilling these expectations when he fed the five thousand, and in John's Gospel it is recorded that the people wanted to turn him into a king. He also challenged the clergy in the Temple directly: his prophetic protests, overturning the tables of the money-changers, along with his trenchant criticisms sealed his fate. His silent defiance of the priests and also of Pilate, although non-violent, was no less potent. The manner of his death by crucifixion was a mute condemnation of the collusion between the Temple clergy and the occupying power.

At another level, and in the grand scheme of the Bible as a whole, the choices that Jesus faced were those faced by Adam and Eve in the Garden of Eden and thus faced by every human being. As "the second Adam", Jesus reversed each downward step of humanity away from God. He rejected valuing the created world more than his relationship with God. He "did not snatch at equality with God"; nor did he believe that God's power could be manipulated. He was not deluded into thinking that in some way he "could become like God" in order to overawe his opponents, even in the name of God. In his humanity, Jesus fought evil on behalf of human nature to restore it to a right relationship with God. He despoiled the devil in the desert, and again and again in his ministry of deliverance of people trapped by evil. He also repudiated the idea that he could force the issue politically or violently to overthrow either the priestly regime at the Temple or Roman military might itself. The earliest Christians followed his example exactly, even to martyrdom, because they saw the cross as the decisive sign of Christ's victory over evil.

The temptations of Jesus not only provide a crucial window into the meaning of his coming and the nature of his ministry in the particular society in which he was set. They also provide a mirror to measure our own society and our own personal choices. We live in a society ruled by consumer materialism: this is a pervasive power affecting every aspect of life, and it is highly manipulative. Its impact on the life of the Church, on education, culture, politics and psychological wellbeing is often devastating, and its long-term consequences for the environment are proving to be disastrous. Built on greed and restless delusion, through advertising, it is the most serious challenge yet faced by Christianity.

Megalomania is also a serious phenomenon: in the last century, millions lost their lives as a result of totalitarian dictatorships, and many live under such oppression today. Closely allied to this were (and are) ideologies that manipulate the minds of people with devastating consequences, not least for those who will not conform. Think of Communism, Nazism, Anti-Semitism and now Islamic fundamentalism. All these mind-sets define themselves to the detriment of others, not least of Christianity itself.

The temptations of Jesus therefore pose these questions, politically and personally: firstly, do we value things more than people, and does our use and misuse of the created world defy our obedience to God, its Creator? Augustine used the analogy of a bride who was given an expensive and beautiful ring by her bridegroom, who then had to go away for a time on business. She should surely value the ring as a sign of the love sustaining their marriage. What would it signify if she were to sell it, however, or to become so fixated with its beauty that she did not notice the return of her husband? If we value things in the wrong way, our relationship with others and also with God is damaged profoundly.

Secondly, the temptations of Jesus raise the question of power and our attitude to it. It is depressing to see how bullying corrupts human relationships and causes acute pastoral problems; for example in child abuse. Bullying occurs within marriages, in the workplace, in school and university, in the life of the Church. It is alarming and sad: what dictatorships lurk behind closed doors in a society that is ruled by freedom within the law? The desire to dominate others is a chronic manifestation of sin, and it was repudiated by Jesus throughout his ministry.

Thirdly, the temptations of Jesus touch on the insidious desire to manipulate the minds and emotions of others, politically, religiously, in education, or in personal relationships. How many marriages have been wrecked by one partner trying to control the other person by asserting subtly that "we are one"? How many children have been damaged by parents or educators trying to mould them as people? The whole child-abuse scandal is a graphic demonstration of this abuse of power, and such behaviour was roundly condemned by Jesus in the sternest terms (Mark 9:42).

So Lent provides a time to check our core values and relationships, and to correct them. Let the example of Jesus be our guide. He came "not to be served but to serve", and he demonstrated throughout his ministry how God values people, respecting their freedom of choice, so that they might respond to him in love. If you read a short piece from the Gospels each day, you will be protected from these fundamental temptations, because in this way you can "keep close to Jesus" and so become more like him in your attitudes, relationships and values. This is the meaning of human salvation because this is the meaning of human life.

1 7

The Unity of the Church

The twentieth century witnessed the birth of the ecumenical movement and a growing recognition that differences between churches should not mean divisions. The sheer diversity within Christianity is its strength expressed in its capacity to become enculturated in so many human societies. How should we think about the unity of the Christian Church?

We can begin by recognizing that any local church organization is called to measure up to the inner reality of Christianity, its moral values and spiritual beliefs. Nothing damages a church more than a discrepancy between what is professed and what is practised. Sadly the Western churches find themselves united in disarray at the present time because of the ineptitude of too many bishops in dealing decisively with clergy and others who abuse children and other vulnerable people. This scandal has done great damage to the credibility of Christianity and to the integrity and effectiveness of ordained ministry within the churches. This is not a new problem, but its widespread incidence in modern times reflects in part the demoralization of the clergy in the face of a secular consumer society, whose values are opposed to and often dismissive of Christianity. To overcome this malaise, Christians have to dig deeper into the nature of the Church.

One way of doing so is to appreciate and learn from the rich and varied history of Christianity over the past two thousand years and across the world. The Church can be thought of as the great tree that grew from a tiny seed, even as Jesus described in his parable in the Gospels. The seed is, of course, the life and death and resurrection of Christ; the roots of this tree run deep into the faith of the Jews as found in the Old Testament: creation, covenant, Law, sacrifices and prophets, culminating in the hope of the Messiah. The trunk of this tree is bound up in the New Testament and also in the Creeds: these support all the subsequent life of the Church and are common to all Christians.

Then from our vantage-point we see a great tree with two distinct risers: the Western one, for many years simply the Roman Catholic Church; then after the Reformation the great diversity of Protestantism in the forms of Lutheranism, Calvinism, Anglicanism; and from Anglicanism various independent churches such as Methodism; and most recently the rapid growth of Pentecostalism across the world. The Eastern Orthodox riser is no less diverse, but more nationally based: Greek, Serbian, Bulgarian, Romanian, and Russian Orthodoxy as well, churches that have experienced vicious persecution for much of their history. Further east, the churches of Egypt and Ethiopia Georgia and Armenia have a long history, just as Christianity spread early through Syria to Mesopotamia, India and China. As you travel abroad and meet Christians in these different traditions, what is striking is what is held in common. The fruits of the Spirit are the same because the rising sap that sustains the tree of the Church is the hidden presence of the Holy Spirit.

This points to the deeper sacramental unity of the Church, which revolves around three points: baptism, scripture, and the Eucharist. Baptism is the common foundation of Christian faith, and that is why as Anglicans we never re-baptize people who have already been baptized in the name of the Trinity. Scripture is the foundation of Anglican Christianity, and so we stand for the Gospel reading in church and should make regular reading of the Bible central to our own life of prayer. Wherever the Eucharist is celebrated, there is the Church. This simple but ancient service has been celebrated every week of the Church's existence since the beginning. This is why as Anglicans we welcome all Christians who would normally receive Holy Communion to come to the altar rail and receive with us. In the words of Paul: "There is one Lord, one faith, one baptism", to which we might add "one Eucharist" too. The phrase in the Apostles' Creed, "the communion of saints", refers to this common sacramental life as well as to the saints in heaven.

The mysterious reality and resilience of the Church cannot be understood, however, without an awareness of the second meaning of this phrase, "the communion of saints". Without the prayers of the saints, it is unlikely that the Church would survive as it does. How may this be envisaged? If we think of a butterfly emerging from a larva, there is a metamorphosis underway in which the insect will depart from one life to another one in which its hidden beauty will be fully displayed. So in the life of the Church, its life straddles the boundary between heaven and earth, between time and eternity, as human beings are being reborn and remade within the Body of Christ. Thus the life, love and prayers of the saints in heaven flow into the life and witness of the Church today. This process of divine remaking, or spiritual metamorphosis, becomes manifest from time to time in the lives of saints here and now.

In the autumn of 2019, the Catholic Church canonized Cardinal Newman, and the Orthodox Church canonized Father Sophrony, the founder of the Orthodox monastery in Essex. Both were beneficiaries also of Anglicanism, Cardinal Newman directly, Father Sophrony indirectly. In our own calendar, there are many more saints recognized than at any time since the Reformation, although we do not yet have a mechanism for declaring saints that might emerge within the life of the Anglican Church. But the existence of saints demonstrates the hidden unity of the Christian Church, because the focus of Christian unity is always closeness to Christ himself. So, in the words of the writer of the letter to the Hebrews: "with so great a cloud of witnesses, let us run with patience the race that is set before us, looking to Jesus, the author and perfecter of our faith" (Hebrews 12:1), knowing that as we do we shall draw ever closer to many other Christians across history and across the world, whose life is on the same track.

Prayer within the Lord's Prayer

One of the ancient creeds of the Church, the *Quicunque Vult*, speaks of Christ taking human nature into God, and this is perhaps one way to approach the mystery and purpose of the whole mission of Christ. For part of the meaning of the Incarnation and the Ascension is being drawn into the love and life of God himself. Christ joins us by his prayer to the Father and to the relationship of love that exists within God himself as Father, Son and Holy Spirit. This is evident in the great prayer of Jesus, recorded in John 17. In many ways this prayer is one of those texts in the Bible, like Psalm 119, which is impossible to grasp solely with the mind— it has to be prayed with the heart and with the aid of the Holy Spirit. One way of approaching this great prayer is to regard it as a sustained exposition of the meaning of the Lord's Prayer itself.

> Our Father who art in heaven

God is our Father because we are included within the prayer of Jesus: "I do not pray only for these, but also for those who believe on me through their word." The prayer of Christ encompasses all those who become part of his Body, the Church. Yet the message of the Gospel is entrusted to the "word" or testimony of those who believe: it is something given and also sent forth. How can we relate to "our Father in heaven"? The prayer of Christ is that we may be found in him, and further, "that they also may be in us": enfolded within the loving relationship between the Father and the Son. Elsewhere in the closing discourses of this Gospel Jesus speaks in a similar way—"in us". This is an awesome thought.

> Hallowed be Thy Name

In ancient Judaism the Name of God was a means of his self-revealing to his people; for in the ancient world the personal name was secret, and it gave access to a person. So when Moses encountered God in the burning bush, it was the holy Name of God—I AM—that was revealed to him, and which became the hidden secret at the heart of the Jewish faith, so holy that it could not be openly pronounced. By the time of Jesus the holy Name of God was solemnly revered in the Temple as a kind of participation in the mystery of God's relationship with his people. In this prayer of Jesus, the Name is something given by him to his disciples: "I made known to them your Name, and will make it known." In the Bible the word "to know" means to penetrate in love. In Christianity we come to know as we are already known by God, as Paul declares (1 Corinthians 13:12). It is through prayer in the Name of Jesus that God is known in this deep and intimate way: "for there is no other Name given among men and women by which we must be saved" (Acts 4:12).

Thy kingdom come

At the end of the Lord's Prayer, the kingdom of God is closely associated with the power and the glory of God, in a classic Jewish doxology. In this prayer of Jesus, the glory is something given to Jesus, and through him to his disciples, as a means of union with God himself. This coming of the kingdom in the hearts of men and women is a process: "that may be perfected into one". It is also the goal of prayer and of our spiritual pilgrimage to heaven: as Jesus prays, "that they may behold my glory". Supremely this is an expression of divine love, which is also divine power, made perfect in the apparent weakness of Jesus on the cross.

Thy will be done

What is the will of Jesus in this prayer? It is "that those whom you have given me may also be with me where I am". To be with Christ in this life is already to participate in eternal life that he reveals through his resurrection. But to be with him may also be painful, as it means embracing the way of the cross—"not my will but thy will be done" (Mark 14:36). It is in the Gethsemane of the soul that this decision is made, not just once but often, in response to the drawing of divine love. This prayer of Jesus was a preparation for his final agony in the garden and on the cross. For God the Father is "righteous", the one whose sovereignty of love must prevail, but with the co-operation of the human will, motivated by self-giving and sacrificial love.

On earth as it is in heaven

In this prayer of Jesus there is a movement out and back, of giving and sending, of seeking and returning. This movement is embedded in the drama of the gospel; it is also embedded in the shape of the Eucharist. How can we engage heaven while on earth? A child once said: "Heaven is a very big place because it is where God is; but the way there is very small because it is in our hearts." In this prayer, we catch a glimpse of the hidden relationship between Jesus and his Father, to which the Lord's Prayer and the prayer of Jesus in the garden of Gethsemane also point. What is its secret? It is "that the love with which you love may be in them, and I in them". Or as Paul said: "Christ within you, the hope of glory to come" (Colossians 1:27).

So we should take to heart and make our own, as an accompaniment to the Lord's Prayer, the ancient monastic prayer of the Eastern Orthodox Church, the Jesus Prayer that embraces his holy Name, remembering that both prayers prepare us for participation in the mystery of his presence and self-giving in the Eucharist itself: "Lord Jesus Christ, Son of the living God, have mercy upon me, a sinner."

1 9

Repentance

"Repent and believe the Gospel!" With these words, the ministry of Jesus opens in Mark's Gospel (Mark 1:15). *Metanoia*—the Greek word for repentance—is one of the most distinctive and potent words in the New Testament and earliest Christianity. It also has important resonance in classical Greek, in the Greek of the Septuagint, and in the theology of Israel at that time.

Essentially *metanoia* means a change of mind and outlook, which results in a turning around of the direction of life in the direction of God. It also implies a change of lifestyle, as the outward consequence of an inner conversion. For as Gregory the Great once said, "The more inward and spiritual the miracle the surer it is." This miracle is the possibility of change in human nature, which is indeed good news. Repentance of this kind is the antidote to hypocrisy, saying one thing but doing another, which was the bane of Jesus' ministry, as recounted in the Gospels. Christian baptism means a commitment to *metanoia* that is lifelong, something that was implicit also in the baptism offered by John the Baptist. Finally, such *metanoia* is not without cost: it entails remorse, sorrow, penitence and compunction. Its goal is humility rooted in truth and love.

The preaching of the gospel is always a call to repentance, first to Christians themselves, and through them to a wider human audience (1 Peter 4:17). Indeed, it is God's intention that people should be given the opportunity for a change of heart, and time to bring it about by his grace: to the prophet Ezekiel God says, "I desire not the death of a sinner, but that he may turn from his wickedness and live" (Ezekiel 33:11). As Bernard of Clairvaux once said, "Life is given to us that we may learn how to love; and time is given that we may find God." As in the story of the Prodigal Son (Luke 15), it is the way back to God that must be discovered and then followed assiduously and irrevocably. In the words of Jesus, "How narrow is the gate and how afflicted the path that leads to life; and how few they are that find it" (Matthew 7:14).

Throughout the letters of Paul and the Acts of the Apostles the consistent call is to repentance, and the early Church father, Polycarp the martyr of Smyrna, was of the view that "for us repentance from the better to the worse is quite impossible". This view is echoed very sternly in the letter to the Hebrews where it asserts that those who deliberately "fall away" cannot be renewed again to repentance, "while they crucify to themselves the Son of God all over again and put him to open shame" (Hebrews 6:6). Indeed this view of repentance as being once and for all and unrepeatable posed difficulties for the early Church to accept, especially in Rome. Could sin committed after baptism be forgiven? This belief about the life-changing nature of *metanoia*, however, indicates how fundamental and powerful was the reality and experience of repentance in Christian life at that time. Lent remains today as the season of repentance, which in the early Church led to baptism and confirmation on Easter Saturday night—participation in the dying and rising of Jesus himself, as Paul indicates in his letter to Romans (Romans 6).

Which leads to the cross: the intention of Lent is that once again Christians should prepare themselves to encounter the reality of the cross, by which all human conduct and attitude is measured, either to repentance or to condemnation. "They shall look on him whom they pierced." These words, found in Zechariah (Zechariah 12:10), recalled in John's account of the Passion (John 19:37) and echoed in Revelation (Revelation 1:7), probably allude in part to the mysterious event in the Exodus story when Moses lifted up a bronze snake on a pole, to which all who had been bitten by snakes could look and live (Numbers 21:9). Jesus himself refers to this in his dialogue with Nicodemus: "As Moses lifted up the serpent in the wilderness, even so must the Son of Man be lifted up, so that whoever believes in him may [in him] have eternal life" (John 3:14–15). The writer of the book of Wisdom wisely perceived long before that this "token of salvation" saved the people "not because of that which was beheld, but because of you, the Saviour of all" (Wisdom 16:5–7). This truth lies behind Christian veneration of the cross.

The cross stands at the focal point of all human life because it determines where people themselves stand, as individuals and as societies, in relation to the truth about God that is revealed in the human nature and suffering of Jesus. Do we stand among the indifferent and the voyeurs? Are we counted among the betrayers and the crucifiers? Do we indulge in the torment of others? Do we actually care about the sufferings of other people? Do we see them for what they are, or do we rationalize them away? Might we be deluded into thinking that such persecution is the work of God himself? Do we collude with the powerful to the destruction of the innocent and weak? Do we, on the other hand, encounter Christ himself in the sufferings and needs of other people? Are our eyes and our hearts open to them, and so to him? For as Dietrich Bonhoeffer once wrote while languishing in a Gestapo prison in Berlin during the war in 1944: "Christians stand by God in his hour of grieving."

What do we see at Calvary? How does it change our lives year by year? Has our life in Christ changed over the past year? That is a question for Lent. Each Sunday Christians see set before them on the altar of the Eucharist this mystery. They also see, as Augustine said, what they are called to become—the Body of Christ. He wrote in these terms about the path of his own repentance: "For love of your love I shall revisit my wicked ways . . . For love of your love I shall rescue myself from the vortex of destruction, which tore me to pieces when I turned away from you, whom alone I should have sought, and lost myself instead in different searchings" (*Confessions* 2:1). He reflected later in his *Confessions* about his own conversion—his *metanoia*: "But during all those years, where was my free will? What was the hidden, secret place from which it was summoned in a moment, so that I might bend my neck to your easy yoke, and take your light burden upon my shoulders, Jesus Christ, my helper and redeemer?" (*Confessions* 9:1).

Paul gives the fullest Christian definition of the nature of repentance—of *metanoia*—in the opening verses of Romans 12:

> I beseech you therefore, brethren, by the mercies of God, to present your bodies a living sacrifice, holy and well-pleasing to God, as your spiritual worship. Do not be conformed according to this age: but be transformed by the renewing of your mind,

so that you may prove the good and acceptable and perfect will
of God.

It is interesting that, in the Gospels, Jesus amplified the Great
Commandment to include the love of God with the mind: "You shall
love the Lord your God with all your heart, and with all your soul, and
with your entire mind, and with all your strength" (Mark 12:30). Indeed
the Greek word "from"—*ex*—implies from the very depths of being, a
great and sustained effort, rather like climbing a range of mountains.

The words of Paul begin first with the appeal of reason and love: there
can be no manipulation or coercion in the call to repentance. He anchors
its possibility in the mercies of God, the deep and costly compassion
revealed in the life and death of Jesus himself. The whole person is to be
offered to God in a sustained and living sacrifice, alongside and within
the acceptable sacrifice and self-offering of Jesus himself on the cross, as
members of his Body. Our life is to be a conscious act of worship that is
consistent with reason, and where everything has a meaning. The only
way to avoid being conformed to this world is to be transformed by the
renewal of the mind—this is the definition of *metanoia*—repentance.

The goal is to come to understand the mind of God revealed in Jesus by
the Holy Spirit (Philippians 2:5); for in Jesus, God has called us to become
his friends, not only his servants (John 15:15). "The vision of God is the
life of a person, and the glory of God is the living person." These words,
paraphrased from Irenaeus of Lyons, sum up the goal of repentance: the
proving through suffering, prayer and experience, as well as by the work
of divine grace mediated through the Bible and sacraments, of the will of
God—something that is utterly good, well-pleasing to God, and perfect.
For in Christianity perfection is a process not a state, at least not in this
life. Jesus himself is the embodiment of the perfect will of God, whose
self-sacrifice was pleasing to God and who was made perfect as a human
person through his sufferings. This promise of Jesus is therefore the call
to and the purpose of our repentance: "If you abide in my word you are
truly my disciples: you shall know the truth, and the truth shall make
you free" (John 8:31–2).

True Priesthood

Lord, who shall dwell in Thy tabernacle, or
who may rest upon Thy holy hill?

Psalm 15:1

The heart and foundation of Christian priesthood is daily abiding in Christ, and it is surely appropriate today to begin with these words from Psalm 15: for each day a priest is called to recite the psalms at Morning and Evening Prayer, so that month by month they become in their entirety part of the fabric of his or her life and ministry. They were, of course, the prayers of Christ, as well as of generations of Jews before him and since. They have been the prayers of the saints in every part of the Church being, as Father Benson SSJE once called them, "the war-songs of the Prince of Peace". They are a sharp and sad mirror indeed of the human heart and experience. For at the heart of priesthood there lies a profound moral duty and therefore a relentless conflict with human nature and with evil. The psalms express that conflict and interpret it to all who take up the call and the yoke of Christ.

Psalm 15 also speaks of the integrity that must be forged in a priest's life, so that by word and example he or she may be able to fulfil the arduous cure of souls. "Walking uprightly" and "behaving righteously" are united by "speaking truth in the heart" and from the heart. How to "speak the truth in love", in the words of Paul? That is the daily challenge before a priest in ministry to others. To be a true priest, therefore, is to turn away from duplicity and gossip, from malice and jealousy, from false values and flattery. Yet how often do these sully the witness of the clergy, often even towards each other? It means instead to uphold and encourage others in their vocation and ministry, clergy and laity alike.

How critical is the ministry of encouragement, yet how often is it lacking? It is about never exploiting people in any way whatsoever: standing firmly and kindly, certainly, but allowing God to act in the lives of others, and at his speed, not ours. For the ministry is the Lord's, and our labour is always "as to the Lord and not to humans", even when put under pressure by others or persecuted. For priests are often subtly persecuted in our society—ignored, disparaged and caricatured in the media. Perhaps there is no more urgent need than to sustain the morale and value of the ordained ministry in so secular and ignorant a society. Perhaps there is no more urgent need in communities today for those who will be true pastors; for if a priest is not a true pastor, he or she is a poseur—and people get hurt. "Am I my brother's keeper?" You are indeed if you accept the call to ministry in the name of Christ, who laid down his life for us all.

The great prayer of our Lord in John 17 is therefore the foundation charter of Christian ministry in his name. In many ways, it is a prolonged meditation on the Lord's Prayer itself, which again a priest will recite daily and often, for and with others. At the heart of ministry lies self-consecration, once and often, to the will of God the Father in obedience to the example of Christ himself. Priests are called in the words of Paul to be "ambassadors for Christ". An ambassador must be able to articulate the will of the one who sent him or her. At the same time an ambassador must be able to understand and engage with the society to which he or she is sent. Their home must embody the values and atmosphere of the kingdom of God. So we remember that in our church, much faithful and effective ministry is built on the life of the home and of strong marriages. Today we recall those who stand with and behind a priest in his or her ministry, as husbands, wives and children, living on the job and in the heart of our society with all its needs and challenges and sometimes dangers too. We give thanks today for long and fruitful marriages, built upon compassion, vision and faithfulness, sometimes through long and dark days of illness and incapacity. For the commitment to marriage and to children is very close to the commitment to ministry—"for better, for worse; for richer, for poorer; in sickness and in health; until death us do part". Both embody the self-giving love of Christ in a continuous act of living and life-giving sacrifice through many years.

This great prayer of Jesus, uttered on the eve of his own self-sacrifice to death on the cross, is about conflict and sacrifice; but it is also about protection from evil, and about God's own unshakeable commitment to those who place their lives in his hands. For the prayer of Christ for us is the only sure foundation for Christian ministry: "I am praying for you" is the message of our Gospel today. What is his prayer? "Sanctify them in the truth: Thy word is truth." To be a priest is to embrace and to be embraced by the demanding love of God expressed in Jesus. Ministry must therefore become "sacrificial because joyful and joyful because sacrificial", in the words of Archbishop Michael Ramsey. The sanctification of the priesthood flows from the self-consecration of Christ himself for us. It means following the "narrow and afflicted way that leads to life"—the way of and to the cross. It is through participation in the mystery of Calvary, at the Eucharist, and also in the heart of prayer, that a person is gradually transformed into the life-giving humanity of Christ—the Body of Christ. He comes to dwell in us as we dwell in him. Can Christ make his home in us, and can we learn, by his grace, to put love in where love is not—sometimes where love is not wanted at all or even appreciated? This is perhaps the hardest graft of the priestly vocation: the daily self-giving and self-emptying in response to the call of Christ and the needs of others that is too often despised, mocked or ignored. Priests are called, in the words of Dietrich Bonhoeffer, "to stand by God in his hour of grieving".

The following of Christ in this way is something poured out for the life and unity and peace of the world. It is a profound and costly challenge to the forces of evil and destruction that prey upon humanity. The duty of a priest in any community is to keep people looking upward and outward: upward to the reality and call of God; and outward to the needs of human beings, near and far. To pray for others is to bear them on our hearts, sometimes to find them almost impaled there in ways that we cannot escape. It is an inclusive ministry because it is to have a heart enlarged, for there are no bounds to the love of God. As Gregory the Great once said, "Your good deeds are evident where you are, but your prayers reach where you cannot be." A priest calls men and women, within the Church and beyond it, to the unity of God's love and to the possibility of sharing in that love in all its transforming power. In the words of Mother Mary Clare SLG: "A person who prays stands at that point of intersection where

the love of God and the tensions and sufferings that we inflict on each
other meet and are held to the healing power of God."

What is Christ's prayer for us today? It remains unchanging as in our
Gospel: "that they may all be one . . . that the world may believe". So in
the words of Bernard of Clairvaux: "Life is given that we may learn how
to love; and time is given that we may find God." If that is true in the
life of a priest it will become true in the lives of other people, known
and often unknown. For to be a Christian priest is simply to lead others
into the love of Christ by presence and example as much as by word and
deed—a "perfecting" of life that is a process and not a finished state. It
is a vocation to life and growth, and also to forgiveness and change. It is
sharing in that hidden work of divine love "making all things new" to
which the life and ministry of a priest must always point.

The letter to the Hebrews provides a profound reflection on the
transcendent meaning of life in Christ, and therefore of ministry as a
participation in his priesthood. If the Eucharist constitutes the Church,
it certainly defines the priesthood. For prayer and worship lie at the heart
of the priesthood, as of the Church, and this is a sacramental ministry
inasmuch as it draws the life of Christians close to and within the mystery
of God in Christ. Christian ministry therefore finds its focus week by
week in the Eucharist; only from thence flows its life-giving capacity and
love, which is the reality of the Holy Spirit. In the bread and wine on the
altar the priest handles that which he or she is called to become in a very
particular way. For the chalice is a supreme pattern for ministry: precious,
singular in purpose, stable, clean, entirely self-emptying and open to
the descent of the Spirit upon the daily self-offering of hard work, love
and service in the name of Christ. Then it is given, given, given to each
person—given because self-giving, and self-giving because of the unity
of Giver, Gift and Giving that is the heart of God the Trinity.

"How much more shall the blood of Christ, who through the eternal
Spirit offered himself without blemish to God, cleanse your conscience
from dead works to serve the living God?" (Hebrews 9:14). Could there be
a more searching clue to the meaning of priestly ministry faithfully offered
week by week at the heart of the Church's life? Today, as we give thanks to
God for faithful ministries and marriages over many years, we touch but
the skirts of the Lord's own ministry in which we are all called to share.

2 1

Mothering Sunday

Faith, family and friends in a pandemic

Mothering Sunday comes at a poignant moment in the life of the Church and society, in the UK and across Europe and much of the world in 2020. It is a special moment when we affirm what we all value most—our faith, our families, especially our mothers, and also our friends. It is hard to recall a time when the celebration of Mothering Sunday, Holy Week and Easter had to be suspended. But the worship of God and life in accordance with the gospel is not suspended, and it cannot be. This is because each person, made in the image and likeness of God, is called to become a "temple of the Holy Spirit", someone whose heart beats with the worship of God "in spirit and in truth". So perhaps the first challenge of this enforced and unending Lent is to cultivate and deepen our faith in Jesus Christ.

We live in a society increasingly preoccupied with material possessions and too often distracted by over busyness and excessive activity. Now we have been stopped in our tracks and confronted with a dire crisis of life and values. We will have time on our hands and real limitations placed upon our lifestyle. So we will have time to pray more sincerely and deeply—for our families and friends, for our neighbours, and for so many whose lives and livelihoods are threatened by this crisis. Pray too for the governments and all who work in the health sector and in social care, here and in other countries. Our faith must be the foundation for all our action, and it must also be the anchor that gives hope to others in a quiet but determined manner. The very fact that we, and others, can no longer worship in church should prompt us to value more deeply the worship that we can give day by day at home.

Mothering Sunday is a festival of family life, as indeed is Easter. Yet this year we shall not be free to forgather in the usual way, and it is very hard to be cut off from our children, and grandchildren in particular. Fortunately we have technology to help bridge the gap, toothy grins over Skype and so forth. As Christians, how we feel for our families is a guide to how we should feel about God, as our heavenly Father, and also how we are to feel towards our neighbours as his children as well. One of the advantages of living in villages is that small can be strong, as we reach out in practical care and immediate comfort to those around us, whether they come to church or not. A strong charitable impulse is a defining characteristic of our country and also of our own neighbourhood; and it is to be cherished and strengthened in the demands of the coming days. As our Lord said, "insofar as you care for others you are caring for me".

It will be hard not to be able to receive Holy Communion for some time, and the lack of this for the sick and dying is a serious concern yet to be addressed. However, we can take comfort from our Lord's promise that "where two or three are gathered together in my Name, there I am in the midst". He remains the Bread of Life, giving himself to us, and also through us, in his great love. Let the friendship of Christ be the secret strength of our lives, and let us be sensitive to his presence among us as well as in the needs of others. Friendship is indeed the bond of love that unites the Church. Prayer as an expression of love underpins Christian friendship. With telephones, we have a wonderful instrument for cultivating friendships, and we now have more than enough time to do so. So cherish your friends, near and far, and give them time. Include within your circle of friendship anyone who may be isolated or lonely. This is a most vital duty as the impact of the current measures on mental health is a serious concern. Conversation and sincere listening are vital for wellbeing; taking an encouraging interest and calling up regularly is so important.

Finally, take to heart the wisdom contained in the epistle for this Sunday from Paul's letter to the Colossians (Colossians 3:12–17). It makes a perfect agenda for us to follow; and it is also an inspiring mirror of the values that already sustain the life of the church at the heart of our communities here. May God bless you all and your families and friends during these demanding times.

Holy Week and Easter

Passion Sunday

Addressing the pandemic in 2020

The readings set for Passion Sunday (Ezekiel 37:1–14; Psalm 130; Romans 8:6–11; John 11:1–45) make a perfect triptych—Old Testament and epistle flanking and interpreting the Gospel reading, with the psalm making a hinge. If we were to read the Easter Anthems in the *Book of Common Prayer* as a second hinge the picture would be complete. This is of course the ancient way of hearing scripture in the context of Holy Communion, as the Word of God is broken and the person of Christ steps forth. Passion Sunday marks the beginning of Passiontide leading into Holy Week itself.

The prophet Ezekiel found himself in a dry valley in the desert full of desiccated bones, a relic of a battle or perhaps of an epidemic. "Can these bones live again?" This haunting challenge now confronts us all in this pandemic as disease and death puncture the bubble of our global consumer complacency, just as it has challenged countless generations before us in human history. Human beings live in the midst of a dynamic and at times dangerous environment. Where is God's purpose, and does human life have any deeper meaning? What are the grounds for hope? For without hope people perish. Perhaps the very fact that human beings need a sense of hope in order to thrive marks us off from other species no less vulnerable to destructive viruses.

The first step towards the answer is a frank recognition that "only you, Lord, know that". The delusion that we are completely in command of our own destiny has to be abandoned. This is God's world and not ours. Only by accepting this does the possibility of resurrection emerge. In the first instance this is rooted in God's work of creation itself. Life—and human life—emerges from nothing at all in its beginning. Human life, however, only truly flourishes when it is energized by the Holy Spirit of God, "the Lord and Giver of Life". The prophet prays urgently that the Spirit—the wind—the breath of the living God—will come into the slain that they may come to life.

The truth at the heart of the Bible is that death does not have the last word, that there is eternal life beyond this life, which can take root within our life now. The promise of God is the only hope for human beings: "You are my people and I shall open your graves . . . and restore you . . . I shall put my Spirit within you and you will come to life . . . and know that I the Lord have spoken and acted." The only foundation for believing that eternal life gives meaning to this life is acceptance that our present life depends entirely upon God for its existence and wellbeing now.

Thus the Old Testament reading prepares the way for the drama of the Gospel reading in which Jesus raised his friend Lazarus from the grave. At the end of the reading, we note how this action of Jesus was the last straw for the religious authorities in Jerusalem, and they made the decision to destroy him once and for all as a dangerous threat, and also to destroy Lazarus as well (John 12:9–11). This is why this Gospel opens Passiontide. Jesus rescued his friend at the expense of his own life. For Lazarus represents humanity in danger of decay and death with no power of itself to help itself, and this truth is also evident in many of the miracles of Jesus too.

The Gospel is also about family, friendship, loyalty and compassion, all of which are needed among us at the present time. Martha, Mary and Lazarus were good friends of Jesus, giving him hospitality whenever he came up to Jerusalem. We read about them in Luke's Gospel as well. What is disturbing is that Jesus did not hurry to the rescue. Their faith and hope and love would be tested to the limit as a result; in addition his disciples had to follow Jesus back into the danger zone, but in a state of confusion as to his purpose. "Lazarus is dead, and I am glad for your sake that I was not there, for it will lead you to believe." Interestingly, it was Thomas who responded first, willing to follow and even to die with Jesus. It would be Thomas whose encounter with the Risen Jesus gives to all subsequent generations of Christians the tangible grounds for their belief and hope in the resurrection.

The faith of Martha as a devout Jewish woman, believing, hoping against hope, in resurrection at the end of time, provided the context for the famous words of Jesus which open each funeral service: "I am the resurrection and the life: whoever has faith in me shall live, even though that person dies; for no-one who lives and has faith in me shall ever die." The word "faith" also means "trust": "Do you believe this?" means therefore "Can you trust me?" The challenge of the present global crisis is therefore one of trust. Where and in whom do we place our deepest trust?

The compassion of Mary opens a window into the inner feelings of Jesus as a human being. "Lord, if only you had been here my brother would not have died." How often has this prayer of lament been said across all human generations: "If only . . . ". Jesus was rocked to the core and deeply distressed, not for the first time, and certainly not for the last. It is the compassion and empathy of Jesus for those facing suffering and bereavement that gives to the pastoral ministry of the Church its unique capacity to come alongside suffering human beings and to care for the dying. "In so far as you care for the least of these my brethren, you are caring—and weeping—for me." It is this hope and belief that also underpins and supports by prayer the extraordinary dedication and vocation with which so many human beings, Christians and non-Christians alike, are caring for others, both known and unknown, across the world. "Jesus wept"—perhaps the most telling sentence in the Gospel, paves the way for "Lazarus, come forth!"—God's overruling of death, here and hereafter.

In the epistle that Paul wrote to the church in Rome, barely thirty years after the events recorded in the Gospel, we can see the impact of this belief on the first generation of Christians, both Jews and Gentiles. We need to listen very closely to their testimony: "Those who live on the level of the old human nature have their outlook formed by it, and that spells death. . . . This outlook is at enmity with God, being in no way subject to the law of God." These are stern words which challenge the false values of any generation, including our own. You can no more defy the law of God's love than you can ignore the law of gravity. If you try to do so, you will collide sooner or later with the sovereignty of God.

"But you do not live like that." Or perhaps, "You should not live like that." So we each face a choice. "Those who live on the level of the Spirit have a spiritual outlook that is life and peace." Why is this so? It is because "God's Spirit dwells within you", and without this animating Spirit within the heart a person cannot really become a Christian. The Holy Spirit brings Christ into the heart of each human life, as into a hidden sanctuary, planting eternal life within life in this world in a way that neither sin, evil, disease nor death can destroy. So "if the Spirit of him who raised Jesus from the dead dwells within you, then God who raised Jesus Christ from the dead will also give new life to your mortal bodies through his indwelling Spirit". As Paul said elsewhere, "Christ in you—the hope of glory."

2 3

Palm Sunday

It is always interesting to read the accounts of the entry to Jerusalem in each of the four Gospels. Mark's account is terse, though much is implied: it was formed when people could still remember what had happened. Luke's account shadows that of Mark, but adds the significant detail that the people intruded the word "King" into the line of Psalm 118 that they were chanting. Psalm 118 was one of "the psalms of ascent" that Jewish pilgrims sang as they approached the holy city, especially at Passover. In Matthew's account, the evangelist cites explicitly the passage in the prophet Zechariah that predicted such an entry of a triumphant king entering the holy city "meek and riding upon a colt, the foal of an ass" (Zechariah 9:9). The entry is closely linked to the action of Jesus in purging the Temple of its traders, noting the fact that Jesus openly healed "the blind and lame who came to him in the Temple". They were normally excluded from major religious festivals.

John's Gospel gives the inside story, linking the entry of Jesus to Jerusalem with the healing of Lazarus. Indeed, in the Orthodox tradition the Saturday before Palm Sunday is kept as Lazarus Saturday with full liturgical provision. For the religious authorities in Jerusalem, the raising of Lazarus was the last straw. They decided to arrest Jesus—and Lazarus also, if they could. This great miracle provoked a tide of support for Jesus, as his disciples from Galilee met those from Judea and Jerusalem, and they all marched on Jerusalem. Was this going to be an attempt at a coup d'état—or would it end in a bloodbath?

This was certainly the moment when Jesus openly threw down the gauntlet to the religious and political authorities in the city and Temple. This prospect hovers over the whole Gospel narrative, from the temptations of Jesus onwards, and in John's Gospel there is an account of similar action by Jesus in the Temple right at the beginning of his ministry. How would Jesus deliver Israel? Inasmuch as there had been a massacre of Galilean pilgrims the year before at Passover (Luke 13:1), this kind of provocation was the last thing the authorities wanted or needed. Indeed, Pilate, the Roman governor, had to be in residence in the fortress within the city of Jerusalem at Passover in order to keep the lid on a potentially volatile situation, if he could.

The psalm that the pilgrims chanted, Psalm 118, is the backdrop to the story of the entry to Jerusalem. It commemorates the deliverance of Israel from genocide and slavery in Egypt. But it is also a song of defiance, as the Passover, which attracted Jewish pilgrims and others from far and wide on pilgrimage, had become a protest against Roman occupation. Psalm 118 is also important for the way in which the events of Holy Week leading up to the death of Jesus were perceived by the earliest Christians. Jesus himself drew attention to this in his last public parable about the vineyard: "The stone which the builders rejected has become the corner-stone." For embedded within this psalm are words that intimate hope and triumph over death: "I shall not die but live." It is therefore one of the most important texts for understanding the Passion narrative.

The entry to Jerusalem and the Temple was thus a deliberate and provocative act by Jesus, and highly dangerous too. Although in one sense he was a non-violent protestor, he also deliberately upturned many expectations about being God's Messiah during the last week of his life. He proved himself to be the Servant-King, and also the willing sacrifice offered to God for the sins of the people. "He emptied himself, taking the form of a servant . . . and humbled himself even to death on the cross" (Philippians 2:7–8).

For Christians, Palm Sunday is the occasion when they commit themselves again to following Jesus as their Lord and King. Indeed, if Jesus is not Lord of all our lives, he is not Lord at all. The character of his Lordship, demonstrated here and throughout Holy Week, should determine the ethos of Christian discipleship. Is Jesus Christ the authority in our lives? Is he central in our prayers and use of time, central also in our use of money and opportunity? Does his example guide how we relate to others? Are we becoming more Christ-like in our love and service of others and in our prayers for them, and in our willingness to seek the will of God and to do it? Can Holy Week be a week with a difference? For in the events of this last week of the life of Jesus the heart of God stands revealed.

2 4

The Mystical Vine

The costly heart of Bonaventure's spiritual theology is encapsulated in this short meditation, which was perhaps delivered as a sermon or a series of retreat addresses. Christ crucified stands at the centre of Bonaventure's thought and prayer. With the memory of Francis still fresh, the words of Paul, "I am crucified with Christ" (Galatians 2:19) resonated in a new way, which Bonaventure tried to intimate here as elsewhere. For it is only by being crucified with Christ that union with him occurs at the deep turning point of the world's redemption. The biblical roots of this extended parable lie in the teaching of Jesus about the true vine and the symbol of the tree of life in Revelation, to which Bonaventure refers explicitly at the opening of his meditation.

He begins by outlining the characteristics of a vine and its cultivation: it is carefully planted, being an offshoot of an existing plant. Christ similarly was the "offshoot" of God the Father, planted in the loving soil of his holy Mother, and cultivated by the Holy Spirit. To fare well, vines have to be vigorously pruned, so Jesus was circumcised, being wounded to heal our sorrows. In another way he was being "pruned" every time he was denied the honour due to him as God's Son. "His self-emptying was a kind of pruning", as ignominy, humiliation and poverty were his lot. "He was poor indeed in his birth, but poorest of all when hanging on the cross", being cut off from his family and friends in the degradation of his death. Often his enemies tried to entrap him, digging a ditch as it were around him into which they fell themselves. Their malice led finally to his torture, physically piercing a heart that was already wounded for love of humanity. "O how good and blessed a thing it is to dwell within your heart, beloved Jesus . . . for Jesus and I share one heart." The side of Jesus was pierced on the cross to reveal the open door into God's redeeming love. Such love is comparable to that between bridegroom and bride, and Bonaventure cites words from the Song of Songs, for "an ardent lover always receives a wound of love". Christians are called to reciprocate this outpouring divine love, given at such great cost.

Vines have to be trained, often stripped down to just three growth points and strung out along a frame. Christ was tied like a vine by his obedience to the will of his Father that was mirrored by his obedience to his parents. He was also constrained within the womb of Mary and confined within a narrow crib. At the end of his life, he was bound as a captive and led away to die. Out of compassion, Jesus endured complete loss of liberty and power. He was bound to a pillar and scourged viciously, tied to it like a vine on a pole. Crowned with thorns in mockery, his shame undoes all human pretension, for faced with the crucifixion of Jesus, who can restrain their grief? Yet nailed to the cross by iron piercings, his body becomes the bread of salvation. "He became incarnate for us, not only to change himself into our human nature, but also to transform us into his spirit." The whole life of Jesus is both an example and a martyrdom. His poverty matched his prayers, for his hunger was the hunger of love. But "who would think to find beauty in the form of his body so desecrated?" Cast out of the vineyard onto a rubbish tip, Jesus was stripped naked to die in ignominy. Who could not be moved by his Passion? Yet by his mutilation human disfigurement is cured, so that we may be "conformed to the body of his glory" (Philippians 3:21).

In the second part of this meditation, Bonaventure reflected on the last words of Jesus describing them as leaves from the vine of life, the cross resembling the frame on which a vine might be hung. In another striking metaphor, the body of Jesus stretched out on the cross was like a strung lute, his last utterances being its seven strings. His words, "Father, forgive them" become the shield of forgiving faith. The promise of paradise to the dying thief testified to complete reconciliation of a sinner with Jesus himself—"you will be with me in Paradise". This is the wellspring of Christian hope. "Mother, behold your son" expressed the deep compassion of Jesus for his mother in her heart-breaking grief, a terrible suffering that compounded his own in his helplessness. Jesus' bitter cry of desolation to God revealed his inner suffering, the spiritual violence being done to him. Yet it reaches out in love to Christians suffering similar affliction and death. Christ's cry of thirst revealed his suffering and also his zealous love for human beings, his desire for their redemption. "It is finished" means "it is accomplished": and therefore the work of human salvation was brought to perfect completeness in Christ's death. Scripture was fulfilled. His final commendation of his spirit sets an example for all who follow him, as they place their life and death into the hands of God, their loving Father. For the blood of Jesus outpoured has become the drink of the faithful in their love for him. Truly "from the first moment of his life until the harsh death he endured at the end, Jesus was suffering death".

Bonaventure then reflected on the recorded moments in the Gospels when Jesus shed his blood, the first of which was at his circumcision and naming as Saviour. He also reflected deeply on the agony of Jesus in the garden of Gethsemane in which his heart was broken by the press of inner spiritual affliction. When the face of Jesus was assaulted by his mockers, his blood was again shed, as when the crown of thorns was pressed home on his head. The scourging of Jesus resulted in further great loss of blood: yet his patience sets an example to all who follow in his footsteps as Christian disciples. For "Love seeks not to spare itself, but pleads for the salvation of its own." Nailed to the cross, Jesus was covered in bloody wounds and pierced through in death, whence flowed blood and water as the fountain of sacramental love and remaking. The whole path of Christ is a return to God, who in Jesus reaches out in love to human beings, calling them to return to him. Contemplation of the crucified body of Christ opens the heart to the love of God.

"Finally, through the door of his lanced side, let us enter that most humble of hearts, the heart of Jesus the Most High. Here without a doubt lies that inexpressible treasure, the true love for which we have always longed. . . . So great a love longs also for you and craves your heart; such love longs to embrace you." Bonaventure's beautiful meditation concludes with the voice of the suffering Jesus calling out in love to those whom he would recreate in his own likeness: "The reason I became visible was in order that you might see me and give me your love . . . I gave myself to you: will you give yourself to me?"

2 5

Why did you forsake me?

Reflections for Good Friday

Darkness and holiness: Psalm 22:1–8

It is striking that Mark's Gospel records Jesus' dying words not in Greek but in his mother tongue—Aramaic: "*Eloi, Eloi, lama sabachthani?*"— "My God, My God, why did you forsake me?" Jesus was remembered as one "who in the days of his flesh offered up prayers and supplications with strong crying and tears unto him that was able to save him from death" (Hebrews 5:7). How does this apparent cry of desolation and despair connect with his life of prayer and inner experience of God, whom in another bitter context—Gethsemane—he could still address as "Abba"—"Father"? What is the connection between his prayer in Gethsemane and his last prayer on the cross?

The psalms were, of course, the prayers of Jesus, and of his family and disciples; their language broods over that of the Gospels to a remarkable degree. It is often true that when a line is quoted from the scripture the whole passage is usually envisaged. If this psalm was on the lips of Jesus as he was dying, does its entirety shed light on the meaning of his Passion?

The Psalms of suffering stand alongside the great passages in Isaiah and elsewhere that portray the suffering servant of the Lord who, like Job, encountered apparent dereliction by God. They form the foundation for the earliest Christian theology. The word "forsaken" has the sense of "being abandoned" or "being left behind", like a child deprived of its parent. Yet at the heart of the covenant stands the promise of God given by Moses to Joshua and his successors: "The Lord thy God will not fail thee nor forsake thee" (Joshua 1:5). The early Christians took over this promise of God as their own. They proclaimed that God had not abandoned Jesus to death, citing words drawn from another psalm: "You will not abandon my soul in Hades—the realm of the dead" (Psalm 16:10).

Through the darkness of Calvary they discerned the continuity of God's promise to those who put their trust in him: "Even though I walk through the valley of the deep darkness of death, I will fear no evil: for thou art with me" (Psalm 23:4). As Paul testified from his own experience as a Christian apostle: "We are pressed hard on every side but not crushed, perplexed but not in despair; pursued but not abandoned, struck down but not destroyed; for we are always bearing about in our body the putting to death of Jesus, so that the life of Jesus may also be revealed in our body" (2 Corinthians 4:8–10). Does Psalm 22 shed light on this experience, this *transitus* from darkness to light, from death to life, through suffering to redemption?

In the words of this psalm, Jesus appealed to the long memory of Israel, to the faithfulness of God towards those who had trusted him. He proved to be their vindication despite overwhelming odds. For God's faithfulness is rooted in his holiness: "Thou art holy, enthroned upon the praises of Israel." The great darkness of Calvary, lasting for an interminable three hours, is of a piece with the darkness of Gethsemane, when the inner crucifixion of Jesus began, as he submitted his will to that of his Father. Is it only in this darkness that the holiness of God draws near to the plight of sinful humanity?

"I am a worm and no man." Bitter words indeed, echoed in the description of the utter dereliction of the suffering servant in Isaiah: "He was despised and we esteemed him not" (Isaiah 53:4). Yet as Jesus predicted: "The stone that the builders rejected became the corner-stone" (Mark 12:10). How could this be? Elsewhere Jesus drew on an ancient tradition from the Exodus story about the serpent lifted up on a pole as a sign that would save the people from the venom of the snakes that afflicted them: "As Moses lifted up the serpent in the wilderness, even so must the Son of Man be lifted up: so that whoever believes in him may in him have eternal life" (John 3:14–15). For as Paul said: "Christ who knew no sin, God made sin on our behalf that we might become the righteousness of God in him" (2 Corinthians 5:21). God loves and values human beings supremely as his lost children, for they are made in his image and likeness. His redemption of them in Christ is the exorcism of evil from their hearts, evil so evident here in every detail of the crucifixion, of which this psalm proved so prophetically eloquent.

Human betrayal, contempt and making a scapegoat are unpleasant themes running throughout the grim events of Calvary: "He saved others, but he cannot save himself!" Mockery of Jesus accompanied him throughout his ministry. This is why the picture in Isaiah 53 of the plight of God's suffering servant seemed so apt when the earliest Christians proclaimed Jesus as Saviour and Lord. For he himself had pointed the way in his own teaching: "Truly the Son of Man did not come to be served, but to serve, and to give up his life as a ransom for many" (Mark 10:45).

"He trusted in the Lord that He would deliver him: so let Him deliver him, seeing that He delights in him!" How unoriginal are the features of original sin! These cruel words in the psalm, inflicted upon Jesus as upon countless other victims of injustice and cruelty through the ages, were intended to cause despair and bitter inner suffering in a religious person undergoing torture and capital punishment. Yet in the Bible, deliverance and delight are closely conjoined: for example, in the baptism of Jesus in the divine words, "You are my beloved Son, in you I am well pleased." The twisting of their meaning into mockery does not rob them of their meaning in relation to Christ, suffering on the cross: for in the darkness of Calvary, "God was in Christ, reconciling the world unto Himself" (2 Corinthians 5:18).

Succour and sundering: Psalm 22:9–21

"Thou art He that took me out of the womb: thou didst teach me to trust even upon my mother's breasts. I was cast upon thee from the womb: thou art my God from my mother's belly." This interjection of reminiscence in Psalm 22 is all the more striking in the light of the presence of Mary, the mother of the Lord, at the cross. This is a unique detail of John's account, placing her among the other courageous women, whose tenacity was not deflected by the fear and squalor of crucifixion. Their fidelity was a gleam of light in the darkness, as well as crucial for what followed after the death of Jesus.

The torture and murder of Jesus stand for ever as a reproach and condemnation of torture and capital punishment wherever it is found. How can the tenderness with which a baby is handled by its mother be transformed into the cruelty that can nail a person to a cross, having first scourged someone to the point of death? Embedded in this psalm, however, and flowing from the cross, is a remarkable stream of compassion, as in the love that Jesus had for his mother, and also for his disciple whom he could trust to look after her.

The mother of the Lord is a key witness to the mystery of the cross. Her path of martyrdom was marked out for her from the beginning: "Behold, this child is set for the falling and rising up of many in Israel; and as a sign to be spoken against: indeed, a sword shall pierce through your own soul . . . " (Luke 2:34–5). Her presence may well have sustained the compassion of Jesus in human terms through this nightmare of suffering, for surely his confidence in God as "Abba—Father" must have had a deep root in his upbringing, and in the piety, love and compassion of his own parents.

Luke also witnesses to this continuing compassion of Jesus towards those around him evidenced in his prayer for those crucifying him, and his concern for those dying next to him. "Father, forgive them, for they know not what they do." This is the judgement of the cross: these words for ever reveal the blindness and insensitivity of human beings consumed by evil and perpetrating cruelty. They remain responsible for their deeds, but they are destroying themselves in the process. Over against this is the courageous compassion of Jesus, fulfilling his own teaching to love your enemies and pray for your persecutors.

In Luke's account, Jesus died with the words of another psalm on his lips: "Father, into your hands I commend my spirit" (Psalm 31:5). This psalm too sheds light on the experience and memory of Jesus at this grim moment of apparent failure and humiliation; in many respects it is an apt commentary on the vicissitudes of his ministry as recorded in the Gospels. It speaks of a sustained conspiracy and policy of social ostracism to the point where a person feels "forgotten as a dead man out of mind . . . a broken vessel". Ringed by terror, knowing that a plot is being laid for his destruction, this psalm testifies nonetheless to a dogged trust in God in the midst of it all, and it ends on a note of hope.

There can be no mitigation of the deliberate intent that destroyed Jesus: the story of his betrayal and Passion is a mirror of humanity in all its most despicable and often typical characteristics. But it also sheds light on the common bond of human need and fragility that elicits an inexorable stream of sympathy and compassion from Jesus even in the darkest place: for "he is able to save to the uttermost those who draw near to God through him, seeing that he ever lives to make intercession for them" (Hebrews 7:25).

Psalm 22 proceeds with a graphic and harrowing description of what it feels like to be tortured to the point of death, aptly foreshadowing the peculiar degradation that the Romans intended by crucifixion. "All my bones are out of joint; my heart is like wax melting into my bowels . . . They have bound and pierced my hands and my feet: I may tell all my bones." The person feels threatened and completely vulnerable, a public spectacle and a victim of cruelty. "I am being poured out like water" . . . a telling phrase that in the context of Calvary takes on a specific meaning and resonance. For in the Lamentations of Jeremiah, the prophet is poured out in anguish for the ravaging and destruction of the daughter of the people.

"I am the person that has seen affliction by the rod of his wrath. He has led me and caused me to walk in darkness without any light. Surely he turns his hand against me again and again all day long" (Lamentations 3:1–3). These haunting words from Lamentations also came to describe the suffering of Christ in the minds of early Christians as the one upon whom "the Lord laid the iniquity of us all" (Isaiah 53:6). He indeed became the scapegoat, bearing away the sins of humanity, dying outside the city gate on a rubbish tip, the one from whom people averted their gaze if they could.

"I am being poured out like water." These words also connect with the unique testimony of John's Passion narrative, which describes the deliberate piercing of the side of Jesus by the soldiers to check that he was indeed dead. For this evangelist, this final act of callousness is both a fulfilment of prophecy associated with the Passover sacrifice and an intimation of divine judgement to come: for "they shall look upon him whom they pierced" (Zechariah 12:10). For later Christians this outpouring of blood and water came to signify the life-giving sacraments of baptism and the Eucharist, the self-emptying of Christ for the redemption of the world.

The seed of hope: Psalm 22:22–end

No one can know how far our Lord progressed in reciting Psalm 22 before he died: perhaps it does not matter as it was clearly a prayer close to his heart. If it were so important to him, then its ending is no less significant than its harrowing beginning. For like the suffering servant passage in Isaiah 53 and other psalms of suffering, this psalm ends on a note of hope. It is as if death and resurrection are both woven into the fabric of the Old Testament, and that it was the genius and purpose of Jesus to highlight this dimension in his own teaching and actions, as well as to appropriate it to himself as the Son of Man, whose destiny it was to suffer and to die on the cross. In Mark's Gospel, there are three solemn predictions of this destiny as well as other hints in some of his parables. In Luke's resurrection narrative, this teaching is a uniting thread running through all the stories.

Words from Psalm 22 are cited in a passage in the letter to Hebrews that in many ways is a fitting commentary on its resolution:

> We behold Jesus . . . because of the suffering of death crowned with glory and honour, that by the grace of God, he should taste death for everyone. For it became him, in bringing many sons unto glory, to make the author of their salvation perfect through sufferings. For he that sanctifies and they that are sanctified are all of one nature: for which reason he is not ashamed to call them "brethren", saying, "I will declare Thy Name unto my brethren: in the midst of the congregation I will sing Thy praise."
>
> *Hebrews 2:9–12*

In some of the early Greek manuscripts, there is the phrase "cast out from God" in place of "by the grace of God". It is an interesting variant that intimates the darkness surrounding the redemption wrought by Christ on the cross, of which Psalm 22 is a potent testimony. The seed only comes to life having fallen into the darkness of death and decay. A dominant theme of the last part of Psalm 22 is encapsulated in the image of the seed—the seed of hope beyond hope, and therefore of life beyond death. Christ as the link between God the Father and his brethren is also found in his words to Mary Magdalene in the garden of the resurrection. Underpinning these two strands in the psalm is the promise to the meek: they shall eat and be satisfied.

In many ways, there are interesting parallels here, as in the resurrection narratives themselves, with the Beatitudes (Matthew 5:3–12). Those who are mourning are comforted beyond their wildest hopes. The meek outlast the powerful ones in Jerusalem and Rome, whose regimes will one day come crashing down. Those who have hungered and thirsted in grief for God's people will be vindicated. Mercy, not cruelty, has the last word. Those perfected by the narrow and afflicted path of the cross that leads to life will see God revealed in the face of the crucified Christ, as happened to Francis of Assisi. Those who overcome cruelty and sin by the path of forgiveness, even at the expense of themselves, will be revealed as the true children of God, by becoming like their Father in all things. By his cross, Christ drew to a head and overthrew the evil persecution of the good that plagues human life in every age, and that leads brother to betray brother and sister to hurt sister.

So today our commemoration of the Lord's crucifixion and resurrection is a continuing witness to the promise with which Psalm 22 closes: "A seed shall serve him; it shall be told of the Lord unto the next generation. They shall come and shall declare his righteousness unto a people that shall yet be born, that he has acted in this way." Only by conforming our own lives to that way of Christ in his life, suffering, death and resurrection can we hope to attain to the eternal life that he offers us in our own generation. For to become truly Christian is to become Christ-like; in the words of Archbishop William Temple: "God is Christ-like, and in Him is nothing un-Christ-like at all."

2 6

Easter Day

Addressing the pandemic in 2020

For the first time in 2020 since 1208, churches in England have been closed at Easter. It must be the first time in history that this has been true across Europe as well. What does it signify? Does it matter that Christians are unable to receive Holy Communion on the principal feast of the Christian Church? Is it not a tragedy that Communion is now being denied to the sick and the dying?

The precedent of 1208 is not a happy one: at that time Pope Innocent III was locked in dispute with King John about the terms of appointment of the new Archbishop of Canterbury, Stephen Langton. The papal interdict which banned public worship lasted for six years and resulted in England being placed by King John under the guardianship of the Papacy, thus lighting the long slow fuse that would in the end trigger the Reformation. Of course, churches have been closed now in the interests of public health; but a dangerous and sad precedent has been set which challenges the basic human right to worship freely.

The unique account of how Jesus appeared to two friends on their way from Jerusalem to Emmaus (Luke 24:13–35) speaks directly to our keeping of Easter in our own homes. We shall be able to witness the celebration of Holy Communion online, but of course we shall not be able actually to receive the sacrament. What we can realize, however, is that the Risen Jesus is able to meet us in our own homes and at our own dining tables. He says, "Behold, I stand at the door and knock. If anyone hears my voice and opens the door, I will come in and we will eat together" (Revelation 3:20). It is interesting that these words were directed to the church of Laodicea that was drowning in its own affluence.

The story of the journey to Emmaus connects directly with our own situation in another way. It is a story about the importance of friends and also of family, and it is a story of hospitality offered to an apparent stranger. One of the most heartening things in recent days has been the outpouring of practical kindness and support to so many elderly and vulnerable people in our own communities and across our country. This unity in care for others is a great grace and a decisive help at every level. The absence of our friends and families is also mitigated to some extent by technology and it seems that the telephone has become a sacramental instrument. We must make sure in every way that we can that enforced absence will make our hearts grow fonder.

In the background to this story in the Gospel, however, is a more challenging theme. Listen to these words of the prophet Jeremiah:

> Our disloyalties indeed are many and we have sinned against you.
> Hope of Israel, our Saviour in time of trouble, must you be like
> a stranger in your own land, like a traveller breaking his journey
> to find a night's lodging? Must you be like someone suddenly
> overcome, like a warrior powerless to save himself? You are in our
> midst, Lord, and we bear your name: do not forsake us.
>
> *Jeremiah 14:7–9*

Bonaventure thought that these words applied equally to the circumstances in which Jesus was born as to this story of his resurrection. Christ comes as the stranger in our midst to call forth our compassion, for "insofar as you cared for the least of my brethren you cared for me" (Matthew 25:40). Our sense of the significance of Holy Communion has to extend far outside the confines of our own friends, families and church communities. The challenge of this pandemic is truly universal, as universal as is human sin, need and compassion. Our prayers have to reach where we cannot be as we think of poorer countries afflicted by disease and death, and as we pray for all those engaged in such arduous work in our hospitals, care homes and communities.

Jeremiah lamented disloyalty towards God, and we might reflect how numbers at Communion on Easter Day have dropped off in recent years, and how attendance in Church has become marginalized as a matter of convenience rather than conviction. How much do we actually value divine worship, and what priority does it have in our ordering of time and choices? Can we still hear Christ knocking at the door of our hearts, or are we too busy? Listen hard—for he is knocking now, quietly but insistently. Make room for him in your hearts and in your daily lives once again.

We tend to associate celebration of Holy Communion with churches and cathedrals. But of course it was celebrated in Jewish and Gentile Christian homes long before churches were ever built. Indeed, in Rome many of the most ancient churches retain the family names of the places where Christian worship began. Although you cannot this Easter celebrate Holy Communion at home without a priest, you can always say grace before meals and you should do so, as in the light of Holy Communion every meal has a sacramental dimension, and gratitude is the foundation of Christian life, worship and family life. You could also revive the custom of saying prayers as a family at home, carefully reading the lessons for each Sunday in advance, and tapping into the many and varied resources for prayer and worship being made available to you online. This is a great opportunity to restore one of the most important foundations of Christian worship—within the home. Worship in church when it resumes will be all the stronger for doing this.

Easter proclaims the presence of the Risen Jesus among us, and this is what is celebrated each time Holy Communion takes place. If you read carefully the narratives in the Gospels, it is easy to see the many connections, as in this story: "Jesus took bread and said the blessing; he broke the bread and offered it to them. Then their eyes were opened and they recognized him, but he vanished from their sight. They said to each other, 'Were not our hearts on fire as he talked with us on the road and explained the Scriptures to us?'" (Luke 24:30–32). Jesus appeared to his friends and they recognized him as the same person whom they had known and followed. The sense of his risen presence and his appearance is always a demonstration of divine friendship for us personally and together, for he says, "I no longer call you servants but my friends" (John 15:15).

We do not know the scale of deaths that may be afflicting our country this Eastertide. I simply point out that this lovely story of friendship restored on the road to Emmaus actually took place in the darkness of desolation and death. "We had been hoping that he [Jesus] was to be the liberator of Israel." These disciples were heartbroken, confronted with the bitterness of Jesus' death at the hands of cruel and cynical forces that were destroying their own society and its religion. It is into this darkness that the voice of the risen Jesus speaks, then and now; our urgent prayer must be that, somehow, those deeply bereaved will hear the words of resurrection:

> God has made his dwelling with humanity and he dwells among them; and they shall be his people, and God himself will wipe away every tear from their eyes. For there shall be an end to death, and to mourning and crying and pain: for the old order is passing away . . . Behold, I am making all things new.
>
> *Revelation 21:3–5*

PART 5

Ascension and Pentecost

The Way, the Truth and the Life

The way to the resurrection and ascension in St John's Gospel

If you are in Rome and walk past the Baths of Caracalla from the Circus Maximus, you come to a three-way junction and bear left along the Via Latina. You then come to the Latin Gate in the great Aurelian walls of the city. But just before the gate, in the middle of the narrow cobbled road, stands a curious small round chapel that was built in 1509 under the direction of the Renaissance architect Bramante. It marks the spot where, according to an early tradition recounted around AD 220 by the North African theologian Tertullian, the persecuting Roman emperor Domitian tried to boil the evangelist John alive in a vat of oil. He emerged unscathed and was promptly banished to the island of Patmos, where he received the vision that is encapsulated in the book of Revelation.

The antiquity of this tradition is marked by the existence of a lovely church called St John at the Latin Gate, which was built in the late fifth century by Pope Gelasius, and restored in the eighth century by Pope Hadrian I. It has been lovingly renovated in recent times and is remarkable for its beautiful tenth-century campanile, its medieval frescoes, and its windows glazed in translucent marble. Its existence, and the tradition underlying it, were for many centuries commemorated in the Western Church on 6 May as the second feast of the evangelist John: the feast of St John at the Latin Gate. His principal feast is on 27 December, but it is too often eclipsed by the aftermath of Christmas. This traditional memorial gives a chance mid-way through the year, and often in Eastertide, to consider John's singular witness to the life, death and resurrection of Jesus.

The opening part of the Gospel for today (John 14:1–6) is often read at funerals, because it contains the promise of Jesus to prepare a place in his Father's home for all who put their trust in him. "I am the way, the truth and the life: no-one comes to the Father but through me." For Jews, the Law of God—the Torah—was often described as the way, the truth and the life. Now Jesus stands as the living embodiment and fulfilment of the Law of God, revealing its hidden truth, and holding out the promise of eternal life. How does the way, the truth and the life that leads to eternal life emerge throughout John's Gospel?

It begins in the Prologue with the promise of becoming children of God, "born not of blood, nor the will of the flesh, nor of the will of man, but of God" (John 1:12–13). The rest of the Gospel demonstrates how this can be. At the end of the first chapter, Jesus predicts to Nathaniel that he will see heaven opened and the angels ascending and descending on the Son of Man (1:51). In Chapter 20, it was Mary Magdalene, who lingered behind at the tomb and who encountered "two angels in white sitting, one at the head and the other at the feet, where the body of Jesus had lain" (John 20:12). In the second chapter, on his first visit to cleanse the Temple in Jerusalem, Jesus put down this challenge to his priestly critics: "Destroy this sanctuary and in three days I will raise it up!" (John 2:19). This saying helps to make sense of the accusation brought against Jesus at his trial in Mark's Gospel. The fourth evangelist here associates it directly with the resurrection of Jesus, noting that "after he was raised from the dead, his disciples remembered that he had said this" (John 2:21–2).

The searching dialogue between Jesus and the sympathetic Pharisee, Nicodemus, in Chapter 3, only makes sense against the background of the vision of the prophet Ezekiel, where he witnessed the life-restoring power of the Holy Spirit blowing over a valley of dried-up bones (Ezekiel 37:1–14). Jesus challenged his learned enquirer with the words: "You must be born again—from above!" Only the Spirit of God can give eternal life, just as he gave life in the beginning (Genesis 1:2). Thus the miracle of snatching the life of the nobleman's son from imminent death at Capernaum in Chapter 4 was a demonstration that the power of the life-giving Spirit was present in Jesus: "Go home—your son will live!" (John 4:50,53). The experience of this became for that family the foundation of true faith in Jesus as the Son of God.

In Chapter 5, adverse reaction to Jesus healing a paralysed man at the pool of Bethesda in Jerusalem provoked a lengthy explanation by Jesus to his critics. He asserted that "as the Father raises the dead and gives them life, so the Son gives life to whom he will. . . . The hour approaches, and already is, when the dead will hear the voice of the Son of God, and those who hear it will live" (John 5:21,25). This would be fulfilled dramatically—and fatally for Jesus—when he raised Lazarus from the dead, as recorded in Chapter 11 of this Gospel. The climax to the great discourse after the feeding of the five thousand in Chapter 6 associates resurrection with the death of Jesus on the cross, and also with the sacrament that Christians now call the Eucharist: the way to resurrection leads only through the bitter truth of the cross. "Someone who eats my flesh and drinks my blood has eternal life, and I will raise him up at the last day. . . . Because he abides in me, and I in him . . . he shall live because of me" (John 6:53–57). Later, when contending with his critics in the Temple, Jesus declared that "if someone keeps my word, that person will never see death" (John 8:51).

So it is that in the parable of the good shepherd, in Chapter 10, Jesus defined his mission in these terms: "I have come that they may have life—life in all its fullness" (John 10:10). His willingness to lay down his life for his sheep is reiterated three times in this narrative, such is its crucial importance (John 10:11,15,17): for the self-sacrifice of Jesus revealed the self-giving love of God his Father. Jesus was not compelled to accept the death that he died: he did so out of willing obedience and love. As the Son of God, he had the power to lay down his life in this way, and also the power to resume it again by resurrection (John 10:18). It is only on this basis that Jesus gives the promise to all those who follow him: "I will give them eternal life and they shall never perish; and no-one can snatch them out of my hand." For eternal life is founded on the eternal love of God the Father manifest in Jesus (John 10:28–9).

It is in the moving story of the raising of Lazarus in Chapter 11 that the reality of resurrection becomes associated with Jesus himself, when he says to Martha: "I am the resurrection and the life: he who believes in me, though he die, yet shall he live, and whoever lives and believes in me will never die." It is as these words are said at the opening of a funeral service that the reality and hope of resurrection and eternal life can begin to dawn in the darkness of grief and bereavement. For the way to resurrection is for everyone through the dark valley of death itself. By following Jesus himself along this way of the cross the truth of the lovely words of Psalm 23 becomes more personal and real: "Even though I walk through the valley of the deep darkness of death I will fear no evil: for you are with me, and your rod and staff comfort me."

"Rod and staff"—what a paradoxical image! Death can seem like such a crushing rod; but in the hands of Jesus it can become, as the cross, the guiding staff along the way to truth and life in him. How can this be? In John 12, Jesus uses a simple parable to intimate how this can be so. "Except a grain of wheat fall into the earth and die, it remains alone; but if it dies, it bears much fruit" (John 12:24). Paul develops this further in 1 Corinthians 15. "Dying in order to live" and "living through dying" become keys to following Jesus, the way, the truth and the life. For this life already contains hidden within it the potential for an eternal and life-giving life of self-giving love, here and hereafter.

Finally we may note the remarkable character of the stories of the appearances of the risen Jesus in Chapters 20 and 21. They serve as a bridge across the centuries for each generation of Christians for two main reasons. They are deeply personal, and they are each in their way stories of relationships restored and deepened—for Mary Magdalene, Thomas and Peter. They fulfil and express the deep truth of this Gospel, summed up in the words of Jesus: "I have called you my friends" (John 15:13–15). The cryptic words of Jesus to the unnamed disciple with which this Gospel closes affirm that the disciple closest to Jesus himself was, as his friend, the authority behind how the way, the truth and the life in Jesus are portrayed in this Gospel: for "in him was life, and that life is the life of man" (John 1:4).

2 8

The Ascension

"One Christ, not by conversion of divinity into flesh,
but by taking human nature into God."

These words from the ancient Latin Creed called *Quicunque Vult*, which is in the *Book of Common Prayer* and called the Athanasian Creed, point to the meaning of the ascension of Christ. For it is only through the humanity of Jesus that his divine nature may be perceived and apprehended; it is only through the humanity of Jesus that God the Father may be approached: for as Jesus said, "To see me is to see the Father" (John 14:9). How is God seen in Christ, and what are the implications for our own vocation and spiritual life as Christians?

Paul declared that Christ is "the image of the invisible God" (Colossians 1:15). This assertion rests upon the principle, found in the opening part of Genesis, that human beings are made in the image and likeness of God (Genesis 1:26). Christ is the expression of God's nature, "the very image of His being" (Hebrews 1:3). Here the Greek word used is *character*. Christ reveals the meaning of the divine image that is placed at the hidden heart of every human person, in their soul.

Firstly, he did so by bringing the presence of God the Father into everything that he did and taught and suffered, reminding people of God's love for them and his demands upon them. The ascension reveals that the whole experience of Jesus is taken into God, etched for ever in the person of the Son.

Secondly, Jesus reveals the mind of God, how God relates to human beings and his eternal purpose for them. Jesus has come to seek and to save the lost: as the creator of human beings, he has come as their re-creator.

Thirdly, Jesus obeyed the will of his Father, right to the bitter end; his will was in loving union with that of God at all times. In Christ may be seen, therefore, the unity of memory, understanding and will that constitute the image of God in each human person.

Finally, it is by the humanity of Jesus that our humanity will be measured and judged by God. All that can stand in the way of his divine remaking of us is our unruly wills.

Paul urged Christians to become conformed to the image of Christ (Romans 8:29). What might this mean? Christian hope is that "we shall be like him, for we shall see him as he is" (1 John 3:2). The word "like" points to "likeness", the other way in which human beings are made to become like God. Christ reveals the true measure of humanity, the full expression of divine love in a human person: for there is no holiness that is not rooted and perfected in love. Thus in the life and ministry of Jesus, his example, his teaching and his suffering, can be seen the full expression of divine love in human form.

Only by following closely the example of Jesus, by willingly becoming filled by his Holy Spirit, can the fruit of such divine love be formed within us: of "love, joy, peace, patience, kindness, goodness, faithfulness, gentleness and self-control" (Galatians 5:22–3). These qualities are divine qualities, and they are human qualities as well. They find their full expression in the person of Jesus himself. Human beings are placed in this world, with all its imperfections and challenges, in order to become Christ-like.

The image of God lies hidden deep within each human person, in their soul. This likeness is often obscured by sin and sometimes it is corroded by evil as well. Christ came into the world to rescue lost humanity. His ministry was one of restoration and redemption, and his work continues in each generation by the presence of his Spirit, to burn away, to heal, to burnish and to restore.

Image and likeness in the original Hebrew are in some ways two sides of the same coin, almost synonyms. Subsequent Christian thought discerned their dynamic relationship and inherent unity. Here the word seal is significant: "Set me as a seal upon your heart . . . for love is as strong as death" (Song of Songs 8:6). To create a seal there has to be a matrix, which determines the form of the seal. Unless the seal is a perfect image and likeness it will not fit the matrix, and it certainly cannot express its character.

How is the human seal to be restored so that it fits the divine matrix which created it in the beginning? Here Paul again is our guide: "Christ emptied himself . . . and humbled himself, becoming obedient even to death on the cross" (Philippians 2:6–7). It is in this complete self-emptying that his profound likeness to God the Father is revealed. This divine humility is the foundation for his ascension, and also for ours in him.

A seal thus reveals two things of great importance: firstly, that it must itself be stripped bare of anything that might impede its union with its matrix; secondly, that human beings, made in the divine image and likeness, are designed to be able to receive the full outpouring of divine love as revealed in Christ, for Christians are called to become "sealed with the Holy Spirit" (Ephesians 1:13). This is an astonishing truth, which the feast of the Lord's ascension reveals. Jesus has taken our human nature for ever into union with God; and our union with him means becoming conformed to his likeness, so that his image within us may be revealed. Only then will the prayer of Paul be fulfilled, "that Christ may dwell in your hearts through faith by becoming rooted and grounded in love . . . so that you too may come to know the love of Christ which surpasses knowledge and become filled with the whole fullness of God" (Ephesians 3:16–17). The ascension of the Lord reveals the vocation and destiny of each human being, created, redeemed and called by divine love in Christ to receive the Holy Spirit and to return to God as to a loving heavenly Father.

2 9

The Ladder of Divine Ascent

"Jacob dreamed, and behold a ladder set up on the earth, and the top of it reached to heaven: and behold the angels of God ascending and descending upon it" (Genesis 28:12). In the Gospel, Jesus said to Nathaniel, "Truly I say to you, you shall see the heaven opened, and the angels of God ascending and descending upon the Son of Man" (John 1:51).

It was the destiny of Jacob, fallen into sin by his wilful deception of his own father and brother, to stumble upon the very threshold of heaven and to dedicate the place as "Bethel"—the house of God. It was the privilege of Nathaniel and the other disciples to witness the risen Christ as the new and living way to God, as in the testimony of the letter to Hebrews: "Having therefore boldness, brethren, to enter into the holy place by the blood of Jesus, by the way which he has dedicated for us, the new and living way, through the veil, that is to say, his flesh, having a great high priest over the house of God" (Hebrews 10:19–21). Now the name Nathaniel means "the gift of God"—a fine description of any human being. In Christ humanity, this gift of God, is being restored to the loving Father, who waits eagerly for our return to him.

The ascension of Christ marks the abolition of "the flaming sword which turned every way to keep safe the way to the tree of life" (Genesis 3:24). The angels that attended the ascension of Christ no longer bar the way to eternal life for those human beings who will ascend the ladder which is Christ's in his Passion and resurrection. "For no one has ascended into heaven, but he that descended out of heaven, the Son of Man, who is in heaven" (John 3:13). The mysterious departures of Enoch and Elijah in the Old Testament were prophetic signs of this ascension. Paul drew attention to this mysterious descent and ascent in his letters to the Philippians and the Ephesians.

The call of Christ is therefore to embrace his humanity, in its virtue and in its suffering, and to follow him along the narrow and afflicted path that leads to life. It is the genius of Luke to portray the completion of the course of human redemption in the simple words with which he concludes his Gospel. "So Jesus led the disciples out until they were opposite Bethany: and he lifted up his hands and blessed them. And it came to pass that while he was blessing them, he parted from them, and was carried up into heaven. And they worshipped him; and then they returned to Jerusalem with great joy, and were continually in the Temple blessing God."

Bethany is a highly significant place in all the Gospel traditions. Medieval commentators delighted in interpreting its meaning as the house of obedience although its true meaning is actually rather more prosaic—the settlement of dates or figs! But it was the last station on the road for pilgrims up to Jerusalem from Jericho, where the disciples from Galilee probably found the donkeys on which Jesus rode into the Holy City on Palm Sunday. It was also a safe house of refuge for Jesus outside the city to which he could retreat each night, for it was the home of his friends, Lazarus, Mary, Martha, and also Simon the leper. As such it was the place of the last great miracle of Jesus which secured his downfall—the raising of Lazarus from the dead. It was also the place where his feet were anointed by Mary in advance of his entry to Jerusalem as the Messiah, and where seeds of betrayal were sown in the heart of Judas. If so, it was also the place of the Lord's most exquisite teaching on a much earlier visit about seeking "the one thing needful", when Martha challenged Mary's devotion as she sat at the feet of Jesus (Luke 10:38–42).

Bethany was also the place of the fig tree which Jesus cursed because it was all leaves and no fruit, belying the reputation of the village and symbolizing the great Temple of Herod in all its temporal glory, whose downfall Jesus predicted and associated with his own death. Finally the village became the place of the ascension of the Lord, his departure from the Mount of Olives, at the foot of which, however, lay the garden of his bitterest agony—Gethsemane.

So Bethany saw it all, in a way: and this more hidden Passion narrative was carefully witnessed by people whose names were for ever remembered, and who constituted a loyal and congenial circle of Jesus' friends. These were the eyewitnesses that Luke valued in particular, and to which he paid close attention in his Gospel and also in his composition of the Acts of the Apostles.

For Bonaventure, the contemplation of the ascension perfects the mind of the Christian. He says in his *Journey of the Mind to God*: "If an image is the expression of a likeness, then when our mind contemplates Christ as the Son of God, who is by his nature the Image of the invisible God, our human nature is wonderfully uplifted and united with him." For "when the mind has done all this, it must still, in contemplating the things of Christ transcend and pass over, not only this visible world, but even its own self. In this passing over—this *transitus*—Christ is the way, and he is the door. Christ is the ladder and the means of our ascent, being the Mercy-Seat above the Ark of the Covenant of God and the mystery hidden from eternity."

In the ascension of Christ, as the completion of the Gospel story of the incarnation, atonement and resurrection, and vouched for by intimate but known eyewitnesses, the promise of Jesus to Mary Magdalene was fulfilled: "Do not cling on to me, for I am not yet ascended unto the Father. Go to my brethren and say to them, 'I ascend unto my Father and your Father, to my God and your God'" (John 20:17). Her impulse to cling on to Christ was to be transformed into a burning love that would follow him through death itself, along with many other early Christian martyrs, as expressed in the words of Ignatius of Antioch: "My passionate love has been crucified, and there is no fire of longing for this life within me: only water living and speaking within me, saying, 'Come to the Father'".

Centuries later Bonaventure captured the same vision and spirit in the words with which he concluded his *Journey of the Mind to God*:

> Let us then die and enter into this darkness. Let us silence all our cares, our desires, our imaginings. Let us pass out of this world with Christ crucified, to the Father, so that, when the Father is revealed to us, we may say with Philip, "It is enough for us". Let us hear with Paul the divine words: "My grace is sufficient for you". Let us rejoice with David in the psalms, saying, "My heart and my flesh fade away: for you are the God of my heart, and my inheritance for evermore".

3 0

The Giver of Life

"We believe in the Holy Spirit, the Lord, the Giver of Life, who proceeds from the Father and the Son." With these momentous words in the Nicene Creed, we embrace the mystery of Pentecost, the feast that we keep in communion with Christians around the world. Who is the Holy Spirit?

The Holy Spirit flows from the inner life of God, as the full expression of the love that exists eternally between the Father and the Son. His presence is everywhere in the Bible, from the story of the creation of the world to the dynamic utterances of the prophets. It was his wisdom that inspired some of the greatest writing in the Old Testament and gives to the whole Bible its unity of purpose. The Spirit enables the love and call of God to come alongside people and to change their lives. How does this happen?

The Spirit of God comes as fire—as creative warmth brooding over the creation in the beginning, as the hot rushing wind of the desert, or as the quiet breeze heard by the prophet Elijah on the mountain of Sinai. Fire gives warmth, for God is love. Fire burns away what is false, for God is truth. Fire illumines, for God is light, and it is in His light that we see light. By the light of the Spirit, we come to a truer understanding of ourselves and of the world around us, for only in the knowledge of God is there any complete certainty. His Spirit subtly enables all our thought and discovery, even if we do not always realize it.

The Spirit of God is also the Spirit of Jesus, his continuing gift of himself to us and to the Church, throughout the world and throughout history. The Spirit comes in order to heal human beings from their sins and from the terrible suffering caused by evil. The oil of his anointing can touch the deepest parts of our lives if we will let him. It flows from the side of Christ crucified on the cross, and there is a cost to embracing the life of the Spirit: for he seeks to be the Lord of every part of our life, in order to make us more like Christ. The gift of the Spirit is therefore the call to become holy. What does this mean?

Paul speaks about the fruits of the Spirit, the signs of his life and love growing within us: love, joy, peace, patience, kindness, faithfulness, gentleness and self-control. These cannot be acted out or achieved by us; they have to become deeply true in our lives by spiritual growth. These are deeply human qualities, of course, with which we are all familiar to some extent in our families and among our friends. But the call of Jesus is more searching: to love others as he has loved us, whoever they are, even our enemies. Are we prepared to become self-sacrificing and single-minded in our following of Christ and care of others? In the life of Jesus and also in the lives of Christian saints we can see what this path of love and self-giving means. Are we prepared to follow Christ ourselves?

If our lives are built on Christ in this way, then it is possible for his Spirit to transform us into the unique person that God intends us to become. Our uniqueness can become a mirror of the uniqueness of God: this is the meaning of why we are made individually as we are. It was Augustine who said that God has made us for himself, and our hearts are restless and our lives are empty until they find their rest in him. What do you most seek at the heart of your life? Where is your life heading to? God became a human being in Jesus to demonstrate how much he loves us—how much he loves you. Can we love him truly in return? This is the challenge posed by the coming of the Holy Spirit. For God is not at all distant; he is very close to each one of us. How do we sense his presence?

The Holy Spirit enables us to pray. In fact, if we will let him, he prays within us, as Augustine also said: "Let God love himself through you." This means that as we give prime time for God each day, as we offer him ourselves, as we pray for others, so his love flows through us. Life becomes a journey into prayer. Life in the Spirit is thus a true education, as he leads us into all truth.

When this happens, great potential is unlocked in human lives, individually and in a community. The Old Testament speaks of the Spirit of wisdom and understanding, the Spirit of sound judgement and inner spiritual strength, the Spirit of knowledge and fear of the Lord. In the lives of some of the saints, we can see how the Spirit within them enabled them to give decisive and creative leadership to church and society in very different circumstances in history.

If the call of the Spirit bids us enter within our hearts so that he may transform our lives, it also bids us look outward to discern his presence in our church and society today. In the Apostles' Creed, belief in the Holy Spirit is linked to belief in the holiness and universal nature of the Church. This is the sign of the Spirit's presence in all the rich diversity of Christianity across the world.

The Spirit is present in the "communion of saints", a phrase that can also mean communion in holy things—*communio sanctorum*. By receiving the self-giving of Christ in Holy Communion we embrace the coming of the Holy Spirit and we become part of the Body of Christ. When this happens, the hallmark of Christianity and of the presence of the Spirit of Jesus is evident in the willingness to forgive and to be forgiven. All of us need forgiveness for our sins. Our world needs a great deal of forgiveness and reconciliation. When we pray with the Spirit, we enable his healing love to flow into situations of hurt, conflict and evil, both near and far.

As Christians we have great hope for humanity because of the resurrection of Jesus. Our human bodies and personalities matter supremely, and this is the foundation of our ethics as Christians: the unique value of each human person, made in God's image, from birth to death, for all are God's children. All human beings are called to share in eternal life with God, Father, Son and Holy Spirit. It is this life, the gift of the Spirit, which gives true meaning and purpose to our existence in this world. As Christians we believe in the Holy Spirit, the Holy Catholic Church, the Communion of Saints, the Forgiveness of Sins, the Resurrection of the Body and the Life Everlasting. So let us pray today and every day: "Come, Holy Spirit, fill now the hearts of your faithful people: and kindle within us the fire of your love. Amen."

The Nature of the Church

One of my abiding memories of a long summer vacation spent as a student in Kenya between degrees in 1974 is of a church which comprised simply a metal roof on pillars, no walls or doors, and at its heart a simple wooden altar. It remains in my mind as a true symbol of the Church: a protected space which knows where it stands, but which has no barriers to entry, at the heart of which is the worship of Christ.

In the New Testament, the Greek word *ecclesia* means a group of people called by God as his own. It relates primarily to the people of Israel; but it came quickly to identify also the Church as the new Israel, made up of Jews and Gentiles following the call of Jesus Christ. From this word springs our term "ecclesiastical" to describe Church affairs; it is also found in Welsh and in some place names in England from the period before the Anglo-Saxon settlements. The word *ecclesia* indicates that what Christians have in common is their allegiance to Christ: this is the basis of their common friendship together, the foundation of their inherent unity.

The word "church" has its root in Germanic language, where it translates the Latin *ecclesia* but is itself a translation of the Greek word *kyriakon*, which means something belonging to the Lord, a piece of land or a building. It can be used of the universal Church or the local church. But the important thing is that the word indicates that no church is an end in itself: it is not just another human society, nor can any particular expression of the Church claim a monopoly of truth.

How then may the Church be conceived? One metaphor, springing from the teaching of Jesus himself, is of a great tree that has grown with rich diversity over many centuries and in many places, so vast that the birds of the air can indeed roost in its branches. Its roots lie deep in the faith of the Jews, mediated for Christians by the Old Testament. Its seed is Christ himself in his death and resurrection; its rising sap is the Holy Spirit so that it bears the same fruit wherever it is found. Nonetheless, historical developments, sometimes conflicts too, have generated a tree with great risers, Eastern and Western. From the Western Catholic riser spring the churches of the Reformation, including our own. From the Eastern riser spring the various Orthodox churches—Greek, Bulgarian, Serbian, Romanian and Russian. It is hard to envisage a whole tree, even from the air; but there are further main branches going East—Coptic, Armenian, Syrian and so forth. The Church is an extraordinary example of unity in diversity; and to be a Christian is to possess a universal passport to many fascinating cultural expressions of Christianity.

Paul speaks of the Church in two distinct ways. He talks about the multiplicity of gifts of the Holy Spirit, reminding his hearers that none can claim a monopoly of grace; rather, each must respect and value what others have received from God. Today, we might think of an orchestra, with its many different instruments, playing together in a harmonious manner under the direction of a conductor. Christ is the conductor of the Christian orchestra: do we follow his lead, and have we mastered the music of the Holy Spirit? What does God "hear" during Christian worship? What music arises from our hearts at prayer?

Paul also speaks about the Body of Christ, the organic union between human beings that springs from and is sustained by the death of Christ on the cross. Christ came to remake human nature, to heal its deep divisions and conflicts. As Christians, we are members of one another, and this truth runs deeper than any denominational allegiances. We are united in compassion for each other and also for human society around us. We are also united with those experiencing persecution for the sake of Christ. It is a tragic fact that today the persecution of Christians across the world has reached a scale not seen since the heyday of Communism. Gregory the Great once said that "your good deeds should be evident where you are, but your prayers can reach where you cannot be". This is why our intercessions are an important part of our worship in church and also of our private prayers—putting love in where love is not in an informed and caring and consistent way.

The Church as the Body of Christ is a deep mystery; its life is sustained by the worship and the intercessions of heaven—of saints and angels. We refer to them in our celebration of Holy Communion: "with angels and archangels and all the company of heaven". Earlier generations were often much more aware of this dimension of the Church's reality than we are today. Yet without the prayers of the Church in heaven it is doubtful if Christianity would survive as it does. "Behold, I am making all things new," says Christ at the end of Revelation. One way to envisage this is to think of a chrysalis: how can something as beautiful as a butterfly emerge from such an unpromising entity as a larva? Yet it does, and to witness its emergence is a miracle of nature before our eyes. So the Church is emerging from the larva of this world, the place of divine remaking, and part of it has already emerged in heaven, resplendent with the beauty of God himself.

So we come full circle to the mystery that we are celebrating, as we do each Sunday, each "Lord's Day". In the Eucharist, Christians see set before them that which they are called to become, the Body of Christ. Wherever the Eucharist is celebrated, there is the Church: in a parish church or in a cathedral, in a hospital, a school chapel, a prison or on a battlefield. The simplicity of divine genius gives us this participation in the mystery of the Church, so that Christ may be formed in us. This is why in the Anglican Church we welcome all Christians who would receive Holy Communion in their own traditions: for there is one Lord, one Church and one Eucharist—God's redeeming sign set in the midst of each human society in history, to sustain our faith, kindle our hope, and to inflame our love of God, Father, Son and Holy Spirit.

3 2

The Good Shepherd

Remembering St Anselm—21 April

In many Victorian stained-glass windows, Jesus is portrayed as "The Good Shepherd" in rather sentimental terms, sometimes with air-brushed sheep at his feet! But this is a far cry from the realities of being a shepherd in the society of his day. In fact, the theme of the Good Shepherd is fundamental in the Old Testament, recalling the nomadic origin of Israel and its founding figures—Abraham, Moses and David. It also cuts sharply, however, as Ezekiel, like some of the other prophets, used it (in Ezekiel 34) to criticize the religious leaders of his day, whose corruption was a predatory betrayal of their pastoral duties. In the end, he proclaimed, God himself would appear as the true Shepherd of Israel, to rescue his oppressed people once again. This chapter in Ezekiel is important background to how Jesus spoke in the Gospels about being the Good Shepherd, and he picks up this very critical note in the opening part of the discourse in John 10:1–8, by exposing those who would be predators rather than true pastors.

Jesus noted that just as sheep recognize the voice of their own shepherd, even when surrounded by other sheep in a marketplace, so Christians respond to the voice and call of Jesus himself, as his relationship with them is the foundation of their following of him. In all the Gospels, this strand in the teaching of Jesus about being the true Shepherd gets a high profile, and it passed into the language of the rest of the New Testament as a distinctive hallmark of early Christianity. When Jesus spoke about being the door of the sheepfold, this had two graphic connotations: of humility, inasmuch as the shepherd would have to crouch down in the ditch while the sheep trotted in across his back, a smelly operation! And also of self-sacrifice, inasmuch as the shepherd would actually have to sleep within the V-shaped aperture in the stone-walled enclosure, as a living door, in order to protect the sheep within the fold from the dangers of the night.

John 10:9–18 paints a sharp and accurate vignette of the ministry of Jesus himself. He holds out to men and women a secure and open door by which they may pass from death to life, if they put their trust in him. He offers life in all its fullness, demonstrating this by his many healing miracles, including those of raising the dead, and driving out evil. He put himself at the risk of political and religious condemnation by his actions towards those in the direst need, and also by his fearless teaching. His ministry was self-sacrificial in its compassion and also in its courage. His care for his flock was personal, based on knowledge of people as individuals, making them objects of his loving attention. He calls those who follow him his friends, as he seeks to draw them into the communion of love that he has with his Father. The test of his authenticity as God's own Good Shepherd was his willingness to die for his flock, to take on the evil that assails humanity, and to defeat it by his own suffering. His mission is therefore truly universal—to all the lost children of God—for it expresses the unquenchable love of God for the world, a love so great that he spared not his own Son (John 3:16). As the mediator between God and humanity, Jesus continues to seek to restore the unity of human beings in communion with God himself.

Faith in Christ is therefore the sole foundation of the Church's existence and unity, and this passage outlines the salient characteristics of the Christian Church. It too is called to provide an open door without impediment through which people may pass, in order to encounter the living Christ at the heart of the Church's worship and life. By its compassion, the Church should be a place of healing and deliverance, proclaiming the Gospel without fear or favour, reaching out in particular to the neediest members of human society. Christian compassion is sustained by a vocation to serve others in a truly Christ-like manner, and such love can never be simply contractual. The spirit of the marriage vows, "for better for worse . . . in sickness and in health", governs the spirit of all Christian relationships, especially the care of the young, the sick, the dying and the vulnerable. For Christians are called to serve others and never to try to control them.

In the fight against evil in all its forms, Christian witness must be courageous, and in some places today this means facing suffering and death for the sake of Christ. The worldwide growth and spread of Christianity is testimony to its universal relevance and appeal, however, as is the rich variety in its expressions in so many cultures, past and present. This spirit of loving self-sacrifice is being put to the test across the world now in the midst of the pandemic, as health professionals, clergy and many others expose themselves to the risk of infection, and in some cases to death itself, in their care of the sick.

Sometimes in Christian history, there arise leaders who embody these truths. One of these was Anselm, who died on 21 April 1109. He was one of the greatest Archbishops of Canterbury, about whom much may be known from his letters and writings, and also from the remarkable biography of him that was written by his English chaplain, Eadmer. Anselm grew up in Aosta in northern Italy. He moved to the Benedictine monastery at Bec in Normandy to become a monk there, and in due time its abbot. After much persuasion he became the second Archbishop of Canterbury after the Norman Conquest, serving with great difficulty the two sons of William the Conqueror, William Rufus and then Henry I. In his defence of the Church's integrity and property, Anselm fell out with both kings, and as a result spent much of his time as archbishop in exile on the Continent. He is now buried in a lovely Romanesque chapel in Canterbury Cathedral.

Anselm's letters reveal his wisdom and humanity: for example, when he challenged an abbot, who had complained to him about the young students whom he was trying to beat into submission. Anselm corrected him by pointing out that to tie a young tree too closely is to stunt and distort its growth. Eadmer tells how Anselm, bored while attending a synod of bishops, had to be taken out and given some theology to chew over before returning in a better humour to expedite the decisions! Anselm ordered Eadmer to destroy the *Life* he was compiling, which he duly did; but fortunately for us he had hidden a second copy.

Anselm was a deeply reflective theologian and a person of prayer. It was while he was participating in the night office of the monastery that he became convinced that God is indeed that Being greater than which no other may be conceived. If this is true, then this reality must be greater than the idea, so proving that God, who can only be defined in those terms, must indeed exist. This famous ontological proof for the existence of God has held its own ever since.

For Anselm, *fides quaerens intellectum*—"faith seeks understanding". He wished, as a Christian teacher and pastor, to demonstrate how what is revealed in the Bible, and supremely in the person of Jesus, may be received and understood as true to reason as well as to faith. He also composed prayers of a personal and meditative character that had a profound influence on how people prayed for several hundred years thereafter. They remain very moving and apposite for use today. We remember him each year as an outstanding and loveable servant of Christ, and also as someone whose ministry, both as Abbot of Bec and as Archbishop of Canterbury, was truly modelled on Jesus, the Good Shepherd.

3 3

The Spring of the Saints

A sermon for Rogationtide

The first great and unprecedented lockdown in England in 2020 was mitigated considerably by the stupendous Eastertide weather, which enabled wildlife to emerge, no longer stressed by frenetic human activity, and which caused wonder at the sheer beauty of nature all around. For nature already keeps its own Rogationtide in May, full of birdsong, as we join to pray for fair weather and favourable harvests, giving thanks for the diligence and care of our farming community and for all their hard work. We give thanks too for the competent organization of our food supplies, and we pray for all those involved in that industry, and in staffing our shops and supermarkets, for their safety and wellbeing.

Rogationtide in England often has another dimension too because, clustered around the Feast of the Ascension, we often commemorate some of the most notable founding saints of the Church in this country. We are the beneficiaries of their vision and labours of over a thousand years ago. They meanwhile celebrate the eternal Eastertide in heaven, the dance of the saints, being participators in the mystery of the ascension of Christ and the indwelling of the Holy Spirit. There is no better way to prepare for the Feast of Pentecost than to remember these five great founding fathers of our Church, whose prayers for us draw us closer to the mystery of the Communion of Saints. I have reversed the dates of their commemorations in order to put them into proper historical perspective.

"We have heard for ourselves, O God, what our forefathers have told us about the deeds that you did in their time, and all that your hand accomplished in the days of old" (Psalm 44:1). Fortunately we are very well informed about the founding of the Anglo-Saxon Church, both from documentary sources and also from archaeology. The story begins with St Augustine, the first Archbishop of Canterbury, whose feast day is on 26 May. In 597 he was sent by Gregory the Great to Kent and he died in post in 604, having never returned to Rome. The king of Kent, Ethelbert, had married a Frankish Christian wife, Bertha, so he was amenable to receiving the missionaries from Rome and giving them some quarters in Canterbury based at St Martin's Church, where they restored a ruined Roman church which became the cathedral, Christ Church. They established the bishoprics of Rochester and London, and also created the monastery of St Peter and St Paul outside the city walls of Canterbury, which became an important centre of education and learning. It was later called St Augustine's Abbey.

We know about Augustine and his companions and their legacy from the writings of two of the earliest English scholars, Aldhelm and Bede, whose joint feast day is on 25 May. Aldhelm died in 709 having served as abbot of Malmesbury and then as the first bishop of Sherborne in Dorset. He was a scholar and poet, who was educated for a time at Canterbury. Bede leaves a much fuller legacy. He lived at the other end of the country at a monastery at Monkwearmouth-Jarrow near Newcastle, where he was educated from childhood. His *History* of how Christianity came to the English is without parallel in Europe, being very well researched and also corroborated by archaeology. He was first and foremost a theologian and commentator on the Bible; but he was also a person of keen scientific and mathematical interest, whose formula for calculating the date of Easter has remained in use to this day. Without his labours the early history of the Church in this country would remain obscure, patchy and remote. We have a lovely account of how Bede died in 735, while dictating a translation of John's Gospel into English from Latin.

Bede's influence on the Continent was as considerable as it was in England, and he is a Doctor of the Catholic Church because of the quality of his biblical commentaries. His many writings provided an important foundation for subsequent medieval Christianity in Europe, as is evident in the career and work of Alcuin, whose feast day is on 20 May. He was born and educated at the important school created at York by one of Bede's friends and protégés, Egbert, who became Archbishop of York.

From there, Alcuin was summoned by Charlemagne to assist him in restoring Christian learning and education across his vast domains. In 796, Alcuin was appointed abbot of the royal monastery at Tours, which became under his leadership an important centre of learning, including the copying of accurate copies of the Bible. Alcuin died in 804 having composed one of the most important early medieval books about the doctrine of the Trinity, which circulated in Europe right up to the Reformation and beyond.

In the tenth century, after the Viking invasions, Alfred the Great and his successors as kings of Wessex gradually asserted their control over most of England. This enabled the refounding of churches and monasteries, many of which had been destroyed. A key figure in this development was Dunstan, whose feast day falls on 19 May. Born and educated at Glastonbury, he returned there in 939 to become its first Benedictine abbot. After a brief time abroad in exile, he became in rapid succession bishop of Worcester in 957, then of London in 959, and finally Archbishop of Canterbury in 960, where he remained until his death in 988. During this time numerous monasteries were established across England which were all governed by the Rule of St Benedict. Most of these survived until the Reformation. Dunstan's political influence was profound as a legislator, but he was also remembered as an artist, musician and craftsman, as well as a holy and loveable person of deep contemplative prayer. His shrine in Canterbury Cathedral became a focus of pilgrimage and a place where miracles occurred in the years before and after the Norman Conquest in 1066.

Why should we commemorate these saints, and what do we mean by the word "saint"? The Gospels give us a sure guide. A Christian saint is a person who makes God real as a loving Father, becoming someone whose life is truly Christ-like in a unique and personal way; someone also in whom the Holy Spirit as the fire of God's love burns so that it can become kindled in the hearts of others, often with healing impact. If you read the Gospels very closely, you will see how this can be true in the life of Jesus. The story then continues in the Acts of the Apostles. For a saint is someone who walks in the way of Christ with single-minded and sacrificial devotion—this is the meaning of Christian obedience. A saint is someone open to the indwelling of the Holy Spirit, whose truth refines and transforms a person during their lifetime. The hallmark of such inner transformation is simply divine love—a deep personal love of Christ, and a growing participation within the love which is in God the Trinity; in the words of Jesus, "A person who loves me will be loved by my Father." It is a love that overflows into the service and care of others.

The heart of the Gospel is that God actively seeks our love in this way, calling us back to himself in Christ, and dwelling within us by his Holy Spirit. A Christian saint demonstrates that this is possible and true, as the key to becoming truly a child of God the Father and by becoming a full human being who is being remade in the image and likeness of God. As we recall the prayers and labours of those who created the Church in this country so long ago, and by whose prayers we continue to share in the Communion of Saints, let us heed and take seriously to heart these words from the letter to Hebrews (12:1–2): "With this great cloud of witnesses around us, let us throw off every encumbrance and the sin which too readily restricts us. Let us run with resolution the race that is set before us, with our eyes fixed on Jesus, the pioneer and the perfecter of our faith."

PART 6

Trinity and Transfiguration

3 4

Trinity Sunday

The grace of the Lord Jesus Christ, and the love of God, and
the communion of the Holy Spirit be with you all.

2 Corinthians 13:13

These lovely and familiar words with which we so often begin or conclude our prayers, either privately or in church, give us a secure foundation for beginning to understand how early Christian belief in God the Trinity is rooted in the language of the New Testament. The earliest Christians were mainly strict Jews who believed in one God, invisible and indescribable, who had revealed himself and his holy name to Moses and to the prophets, as the Old Testament records. How could they come to believe that within the very being of this one God there are three persons to be addressed as Father, Son and Holy Spirit? The closing words of the prologue of John's Gospel provide an important clue. "No-one has seen God at any time: God the only-begotten, the Son who is in the heart of the Father, he has expressed him" (John 1:18).

"The grace of the Lord Jesus Christ". In many ways, these words sum up the whole gospel: the belief that "grace and truth have come through Jesus Christ" (John 1:17). In various ways, the earliest disciples came to realize that Jesus as Messiah was also the Son of God, revealing his presence and nature in a unique and life-transforming way. Thus to use the words "grace" and "Lord" was to attribute divine significance to the person of Jesus. His many miracles demonstrated, for those with eyes to see, the outpouring of divine grace as love and compassion. On the holy mountain of the transfiguration, those closest to him glimpsed his divine glory. In the privacy of her home, Mary, the mother of the Lord, became privy to the mystery of his coming. In the resurrection,

Jesus was revealed to be the Lord of life and death, endowed with divine power and authority, the one in whose name the mission of the Church would proceed. The grace of the Lord Jesus Christ therefore constitutes a profound and distinctive prayer, and comparable words can be seen elsewhere at the end of some of Paul's letters.

"The Love of God". These words sum up what Jesus revealed about the nature of God, as well as his own relationship with him as his Father. His acts of compassion and many of his parables sought to convey the reality and demands of the love of God, and his power and desire to make all things new. Christian belief in God the Trinity has its foundation in the relationship that Jesus had with his Father, a relationship into which he calls his disciples, then and now, to enter and participate, even using the distinctive, intimate and personal mode of address that he used for "Father"—"Abba". In the opening of the Lord's Prayer, we are each bidden to pray to "Our Father". In the great prayer of Jesus in John 17, he prays to his Father in these words: "I made known to them your Name, and will make it known, so that the love with which you love me may be in them, and I in them" (John 17:26). A little earlier in the same context in John's Gospel, Jesus said, "if a person loves me, he will keep my word; and my Father will love him: and we will come to him and make our dwelling with him" (John 14:23). How can this be?

"The Communion (or fellowship) of the Holy Spirit". These words point to the answer to the question first asked by Mary, the mother of the Lord, to the angel Gabriel (Luke 1:34), and the angel's answer points the way: "The Holy Spirit will come upon you and the power of the Most High will overshadow you." The unique experience of Mary in the incarnation of Christ points to the mystery which Paul describes as, "Christ within you, the hope of glory" (Colossians 1:27). In fact, the letters of the New Testament, along with the Acts of the Apostles, all testify in various ways to the reality of the Holy Spirit dwelling within the lives of individual Christians in such a way as to constitute a new human fellowship. As Paul said, "It is because you are children that God has sent forth the Spirit of his Son into our hearts, crying 'Abba—Father'" (Galatians 4:6). Thus "The Spirit bears witness with our own spirit that we are indeed children of God" (Romans 8:16). This belief also becomes the distinctive foundation for Christian ethics, expressed in these challenging words of Paul once again: "Do you not realize that your body is the sanctuary of the Holy Spirit, who is within you as the gift of God?" (1 Corinthians 6:19). The fact that each human person is made uniquely in the image and likeness of God is the reason why Christians uphold tenaciously the sanctity of each human life.

Perhaps the most eloquent testimony to the nature of our communion with God the Trinity is to be found in the first letter of John. "Beloved, let us love one another, for love is of God; and everyone who loves is begotten of God and knows God. A person who does not love does not know God: for God is love" (1 John 4:7–8). "God is love"—this is the master-key for beginning to understand and relate to the reality of God the Trinity. What is the nature of divine love?

Only in the light of the example, teaching and person of Jesus can we begin to see how divine love by its very nature finds complete self-expression in another person, as such generous love cannot exist in a solitary state. Only complete self-giving can achieve the full self-expression of love, and that full self-expression is not complete until it participates in further mutual self-giving that is complete, equal and united. The Father is fully expressed in the Son, and the Father is therefore the sole fountain-head of the Trinity that is God. The Holy Spirit flows from Father and Son together as the supreme and perfect expression of the fullness of divine love.

In a Christian marriage, something of this mystery may be glimpsed, as husband and wife give to each other the full devotion of their life in irreversible love and self-giving for a lifetime. From this love there may flow by the grace of God the gift of children, whose existence is sought and cherished equally and fully by each parent. In the incarnation of Christ, divine love flows out in generous self-giving to embrace the created world and to redeem and restore human beings, who are each made in the divine image and likeness. Human beings are made supremely for this love—this is their most distinctive characteristic—and this is also the basis for the profound affinity that exists between each individual person and God himself. In Christ, human beings are called to accept the loving embrace of God in the remaking of their lives, so that they become temples fit to receive the indwelling of his Spirit. In this way, their fellowship within the Body of Christ is being built up. Let us therefore make our own this daily prayer, which expresses the heart of the mystery of the Trinity and also our own vocation as Christians: "May the grace of our Lord Jesus Christ, the love of God, and the communion of the Holy Spirit be with us all. Amen."

3 5

Constraining Love

"The love of Christ constrains us" (2 Corinthians 5:6–17). It is in 2 Corinthians, and also in Philippians, that Paul gives vivid glimpses of his own personal experience of what he describes as life in Christ. In fact, the Greek word for "to constrain" has a range of meanings, all of which embrace the experience of Paul. Here it means primarily "to impel"—not "to compel"; and there is an important difference, inasmuch as "to impel" requires the active co-operation of the will, it is not something to be forced. It is the death of Christ on the cross that impels the mission of Paul, as is evident throughout his letters. Only love for Christ crucified can redeem a human soul.

The Greek word to constrain means firstly to sustain and to hold something together. Paul discovered that, whether he liked it or not, his life was held in the hands of God. In fact, he collided with them on the road to Damascus; and he discovered that these are the wounded hands of Christ: "Saul, Saul, why are you persecuting me?" Thereafter he knew keenly that his whole life was a venture of faith, breaking fresh ground as a Christian missionary, called to bring the gospel far and wide into communities often very far removed from his own strict Jewish origins. He alludes to this in the words, "knowing the fear of the Lord, we persuade people". He cannot compel belief, but he can try to impel people towards Christ crucified, to urge them to become reconciled to God.

The Greek word also means to take charge of someone and to command their obedience. This certainly happened to Paul. He found himself between two worlds, Jewish and Gentile, hardly a comfortable place. He was open to persecution by orthodox Jews, and he was hardly *persona grata* with some of the Jewish Christians in Jerusalem, many of whose families he had helped to persecute before his own conversion.

Now, as he says, "our aim is to be well-pleasing" to the Lord alone. For Christ was the Lord of his life and of his obedience. Paul's was the "narrow and afflicted way" that leads to life in Christ.

Part of the price of Paul's mission and vocation was to be subject to appalling pressures, and not just those of persecution. They arose also in terms of the development of his own belief and understanding as a Jewish Christian, and also in terms of his priorities. He might want "to be absent from the body to be present with the Lord", but this was not in his gift, as he recognized in his letter to the Philippians. The word "constrain" takes on added force here, intimating the pain of difficult choices, of sacrifices made, and sufferings endured, of which he speaks clearly elsewhere in 2 Corinthians. He says, "we are of good courage": Paul needed good courage!

The word in Greek "to constrain" also carries the meaning "to be preoccupied or absorbed". This also is true of Paul inasmuch as he gives us such a valuable insight into his own spiritual experience. His life proved to be a crucible in which the fire of the Holy Spirit was remaking him. "If anyone is in Christ, there is a new creation underway: old things are passing away; behold, they are becoming new." To become a Christian is a continuing process of divine remaking and perfecting, never complete in this life, but holding out a promise of eternal fulfilment in Christ: "for we walk by faith, not by sight". Paul gave to Christianity some of its most potent spiritual vocabulary. Church Fathers, monastic teachers and medieval theologians all referred to him solely as "the Apostle", such was his spiritual authority, and his language has found its way into our liturgy.

Paul therefore urges all who hear or read his letters to pursue the way of Christ, the way of the cross, with determination and single-minded commitment. To be constrained by the love of Christ is also to become filled with his compassion for those for whom he died. "One died for all, therefore all have died: and he died for all so that they who live should no longer live unto themselves, but unto him who for their sakes died and rose again." These are momentous words: for all human beings are children of God for whom Christ died. This perception must govern all Christian evangelization: "We beseech you on behalf of Christ to be reconciled to God." It must also govern all Christian ethics, for it is supremely a "ministry of reconciliation" that springs from the death of Christ on the cross, and which is about forgiveness, freedom and love—a "new creation" indeed.

3 6

The Body of Christ

A sermon for Corpus Christi

Since the fourteenth century, the Catholic Church has observed Thursday after Trinity Sunday as the Feast of Corpus Christi, and Anglicans have increasingly done so again in recent years. It is the first moment outside Eastertide in which there can be further reflection on the central significance of the Eucharist itself within the life of the Church, and also in the lives of individual Christians. Maundy Thursday marks the first Lord's Supper in the context of the Passover and on the eve of Christ's own death. Corpus Christi turns our minds to consider what we mean by "The Body of Christ". The celebration of Corpus Christi sprang from the vision and determination of a remarkable nun, Juliana of Liège, who died in 1258. The great hymns *Lauda Sion, Pange Lingua* and *Tantum Ergo* that are associated with this feast are attributed to Thomas Aquinas, who composed them in the middle of the thirteenth century.

The first thing to say about "the Body of Christ" is that it signifies the life of the Church, gathered round the service of Holy Communion. Where the Eucharist is celebrated, there is the Church in any place and time. Our buildings exist to facilitate this, though at present they remain closed; and as a result the sacrament is being sadly denied to most Christians in a quite unprecedented way. Perhaps this is an added impetus to meditate on the significance of "the Body of Christ", so that when we come again to receive Holy Communion, we shall be better prepared, and never take it for granted.

Paul in particular developed the sense of the Body of Christ to account for two things in early Christianity. The first was the sense that by receiving Holy Communion, a Christian is united to Christ as a member along with others of his Body. "We who are many are one bread, one body for we all partake of the one bread" (1 Corinthians 10:17). This is the foundation for being a Christian. The second was the perception that the many different and diverse members of the Christian Church of different races each find their unique individual role together within the organic functioning of the whole body of the Church, just as happens every day in our own physical bodies. "As the body has many members and all are members of that body; so also is Christ" (1 Corinthians 12:12). All are needed and each person is of equal value, even if not of equal capacity. So the Feast of Corpus Christi recalls us to our deep unity in Christ, and therefore with other Christians across the world and throughout history. This is why in the Church of England we welcome all who would normally receive Communion in their own church to receive it with us. "There is one Body and one Spirit, even as you were called in the one hope of your calling; one Lord, one Faith, one Baptism, one God and Father of all, who is over all, and through all, and in all" (Ephesians 4:5–6).

Clearly Christian devotion towards the actual sacrament of the Lord's Body and Blood sprang from this deep bond of unity and love. "The cup of blessing that we bless, is it not a participation [or communion] in the blood of Christ? The bread that we break, is not a participation [or communion] in the Body of Christ?" (1 Corinthians 10:16). These words have found their way into Anglican liturgy at the breaking of bread and just before receiving Communion. Paul's conviction is confirmed by words found in the sixth chapter of St John's Gospel, at the end of the great discourse of Jesus after the feeding of the five thousand:

> Truly I say to you, unless you eat the flesh of the Son of Man and drink his blood you have no life in you. A person who eats my flesh and drinks my blood has eternal life, and I will raise him up on the last day. For my flesh is true food and my blood is true drink. Someone who eats my flesh and drinks my blood abides in me, and I in him.
>
> *John 6:53–6*

These remarkable words are the foundation for all genuine veneration of Christ present in the Eucharist, and it thus becomes the mediating sign of the means of his grace and the hope of glory. In different ways, Christians have sensed and articulated the real and personal presence of Christ, as he gives himself to us in Holy Communion. This is why we should never receive Communion without sincere and careful preparation; and nothing should ever happen in a service which might distract from the awesome and holy reality of the celebration of this sacrament. The Eucharist is the hidden miracle at the heart of Christianity.

Holy Communion turns our focus each week to the reality of the Body of Christ—towards the human flesh of Christ and the grim reality of his sufferings. "This is my Body that is given for you: do this in remembrance of me. . . . This cup is the new covenant in my blood, which is poured out for you" (Luke 22:19-20). Paul echoed these words as he had received them, as an already established tradition within the first generation of Christians: "This is my body which is broken for you" (1 Corinthians 11:24). This is why the cross stands so centrally in Western Christian churches, both Catholic and Anglican. For just as the lips of the prophet Isaiah were cleansed by a living coal from the altar of God brought to him by an angel in the Temple, so our lives are cleansed by the fire of divine love hidden within the bread and wine of Holy Communion. It is in recognition of this awesome reality that we join with the angels in proclaiming the words: "Holy! Holy! Holy! Lord God of Hosts: the fullness of the whole earth is His glory!" (Isaiah 6:3).

Reflection on the life-giving suffering of Jesus in his body on the cross should also draw us more deeply into his loving embrace. In Western Christianity, there has always been a deep devotion in love and empathy towards the suffering of Christ in his human body. It has coloured the way in which the crucifixion has been portrayed, and it has also found expression in prayers, hymns and poetry of great sensitivity and beauty. Listen to these words of Bonaventure in his meditation called *The Mystical Vine*, who was a close follower of Francis of Assisi:

> Who would not love a heart so wounded? Who could fail to respond to a heart so loving? Who would not embrace a heart so pure? The lover [or Christian] thus wounded, who is herself wounded by love, should cry, "I am wounded with love!" (Song of Songs 2:5). The loving Bridegroom (i.e. Christ) accepts the

return of love from anyone who says to him, "Tell my beloved that I languish for love of him" (Song of Songs 5:8).

Mention of Francis of Assisi directs our thoughts to another dimension of the Body of Christ. When Francis received the stigmata at La Verna in Italy towards the end of his life, it was because throughout his life he had drawn so close to the reality of Christ's sufferings in the poor and the lepers. His conformity to Christ's sufferings was set in train by his embrace of a leper as a young man. His empathy became profoundly developed, as in his loving compassion he and his companions, including Clare of Assisi, sought to serve Christ in poverty and humility, remembering and taking to heart the words of Jesus: "Insofar as you cared for the least of my brethren you were caring for me" (Matthew 25:40). Much earlier, John Chrysostom, as Archbishop of Constantinople in the fourth century, criticized fashionable Christians, who would lavish great wealth on the fittings of churches—mosaics, gold and silver vessels, silk hangings—but pass in and out of church quite indifferent to the poor beggars propped up outside the door. He challenged them, saying that "it is there that you have Christ's altar!"

To ignore Christ in the poor and disadvantaged is the highest scandal and a denial of the meaning of the Eucharist. This is why in South Africa, during the period of apartheid, Anglican clergy were sent to prison for receiving blacks, whites and coloureds at the same altar for Holy Communion. For as Paul said, "You are all children of God through faith in Jesus Christ. . . . There can therefore be neither Jew nor Greek, slave nor free, male nor female, for you are all one in Jesus Christ" (Galatians 3:26,28). Thus commitment to the meaning of the Eucharist and to the reality of the Body of Christ underpins all Christian ethics, personal and social. "Let the peace of Christ rule in your hearts, to which you were called within the one body, and be thankful" (Colossians 3:15). The word Eucharist means thanksgiving in Greek, and it is in this spirit that the Feast of Corpus Christi is best observed.

3 7

Perfection in Imperfection

The Birth of John the Baptist—24 June

Running through Luke's account of the birth of John the Baptist is a very strong sense of providence, acting in a way consistent with some of the most fundamental stories in the Old Testament. The opening verses of Luke's Gospel therefore repay close examination. The irony of the dating of the story to the days of King Herod of Judea is profound, for he was notoriously corrupt, and cruel too, as Matthew's Gospel relates with regard to the massacre of the children of Bethlehem. Yet in so unpromising and compromised an environment, under the heel of foreign occupation by the Romans with whom Herod had cut a deal, God acted.

In sharp contrast, therefore, is the faithfulness and devotion of Zacharias and Elizabeth, their ancestral descent identifying them with the tribes from whom the priests of Israel were drawn: "They were both righteous before God, walking in all the commandments and ordinances of the Lord, and blameless." This is an important, indeed a crucial assertion. For whatever God was to accomplish perfected the devotion of Israel; it did not supersede it. Their tenacity, and that of others like them, was not in vain.

Yet they had no children. They embodied the highest form of marriage in Israel, a priest and his wife; but her barrenness was their cross. Like Sarah and Hannah long before, their home, empty of children, mocked their piety and faithfulness. The years wound on: they remained faithful to their marriage vows, and Zacharias to his priestly duties. How could God act now? He may have rescued Sarah, who was also too old to have children—but that was long ago.

Luke describes graphically, and perhaps from first-hand knowledge, the ordered duties of Zacharias in the Temple as he executed the priest's office before God, entering with the offering of incense into the Holy Place. Notice also the faithfulness of the people at worship: the priest was not alone, he was their representative in the presence of God; their presence was his support. Once again the worship of Israel was being vindicated: for simply and sincerely being in the presence of God is the prelude to any divine intervention.

The worship of Israel, like that of Christianity, is part of something much bigger—the heavenly worship of the angels, which the prophet Isaiah glimpsed in his famous vision: "Holy, Holy, Holy, is the Lord God of Hosts." As Christians utter those awesome words during the consecrating prayer of the Eucharist, the presence of angels may sometimes be sensed, though rarely seen. But on this occasion, the priest Zacharias discovered that as he was offering incense on his side of the altar, the angel of the Lord was standing on the right-hand side, worshipping God along with him.

His fear and apprehension arose from his worship, for long devotion heightens sensitivity to God's presence, direct or indirect, in this case through an angel. First and foremost this is a wonderful case of prayer being answered after so many long, faithful and tearful years, shared by both parents, for Elizabeth is a hidden mover in this story too. The promise of a son constituted the highest blessing for devout Jews. The designation of his name—John—fulfilled the assertion of the prophet Isaiah: "The Lord called me from the womb; from within my mother he uttered my name." It signifies to us the unique significance of the human foetus and therefore of any mother's pregnancy.

The promise of joy and gladness echoes the very name of Isaac, which means "laughter". Isaac also was named by God to Abraham before he was born. But laughter can be two-edged; Sarah's laughter at the promise of the angels who visited her and Abraham was noted by God despite her denials. "Is anything too hard or wonderful for the Lord?" This challenge will prove the leitmotiv of the subsequent story of the visit of the same angel—Gabriel—to Mary.

The prophecy by the angel as to the character of the child to be born is also highly significant: for "he shall be great in the sight of the Lord". He would be an ascetic, someone filled with the Holy Spirit "even from his mother's womb". His life would be holy, the work of God, from his conception until his squalid execution by Herod's descendant. It would all be held within the hand of God.

Hidden in the deserts of Judea, but with the support of his family, until "the day of his manifestation to Israel", the child became a holy man, an intercessor with God; someone who could "come nigh before his face" and then go forth "in the spirit and power of Elijah". His role would be to prepare the people for God's intervention. His call to repentance would be the means of renewal that would unite the true people of God across the generations, calling "the disobedient to walk in the wisdom of the just". In him the whole prophetic ministry of Israel would be focused with a decisive impact, for he would have a key role in preparing Jesus himself and his closest disciples for their mission.

Zacharias' hesitation and questioning was inevitable: "How can this thing be?" The angel's message silences him, quite literally, as a sign that he has had a divine encounter, as well as a reproach for his own understandable reserve in accepting this good news. Gabriel introduced himself by name as a token of his authority, and for a reason that will become clear in the story of the annunciation. So the priest's privacy was blown, and the waiting people in the Temple could see that something mysterious had happened to him during his long delay within the sanctuary, for the glory of the Lord was still present in his Temple. Zacharias' ministry continued for its due time, eloquent in its silence. For he had been silenced by Silence.

On his return home, Zacharias and his wife slept together, and Elizabeth indeed conceived. But she too hid herself for five months, in shame perhaps for her many years of suffering now that "the Lord had taken away her reproach among men"; but perhaps because this pregnancy was too good to be true—or to be lost. The subsequent arrival of her young kinswoman, Mary, was when Elizabeth's pregnancy was well established at six months; and the child quickened in the womb at her arrival.

Joy marked this moment for both women in an age when pregnancy was so precarious. "Blessed art thou among women, and blessed is the fruit of thy womb!" For both women, suffering and love were interwoven in their motherhood, and in their love of God. It is, of course, within the story of Zacharias and Elizabeth that the story of the annunciation to

Mary is enfolded; for all these family stories were deeply personal and private, at the time and for long afterwards. Mary's presence and support was with Elizabeth until her pregnancy came to term and her own was well underway.

Thus the child was safely delivered to the delight of family and friends: "They heard that the Lord had magnified his mercy towards her, and they rejoiced with her." At his circumcision on the eighth day, he was to be named after his father, Zacharias. His mother's refusal withstood the dictates of custom and tribe: "There is none of your kindred called by this name—John!" Her testimony sprang from the depth of their marriage relationship: she spoke for her husband—and for the angel too. Her experience vindicated the meaning of her name, which means "God has promised". As Zacharias wrote the name "John", which means "God is gracious", on the wax tablet, he could speak again: his silence was ended and his first words were of praise and blessing towards God, the giver of good.

For the people around in the hill villages of Judea, the past had become the present: this was a miraculous birth of a first-born son of the same order as those that had occurred before at the heart of Israel's experience— notably Isaac and Samuel. Note that the people remembered it all: for it is upon these local memories, as well as the intimate testimonies of the families of John and Jesus, that Luke rested his authority many years later.

John's life, however, would be haunted by the words with which his birth was greeted: "What then shall this child be?" From the beginning of his childhood, "the hand of the Lord was with him", as would also be true of Jesus. The closeness of God to children is thus demonstrated. John "grew strong in spirit"—his own, and in due time God's Spirit as well. His formation in the desert was not remote from his own family, however; nor was it incongruous with what is now known about the Essenes and the community that generated and preserved the Dead Sea Scrolls.

Thus with meticulous care, Luke has placed this deeply private memory of two named individuals, Zacharias and Elizabeth, within the solemn framework of the covenant purpose of God towards his people Israel. With every resonance of the Old Testament, the hand of the Lord was revealed, as he who works out his perfect purpose within the imperfections of those whose lives were built upon the foundations of devotion and worship, embodying the law of the Lord that alone can lead to life.

3 8

The Challenge to St Peter

29 June

The last chapter of John's Gospel is one of the most interesting passages in all the Gospels. It seems to stand as a deliberate appendix after the formal ending of the Gospel, and it was almost certainly written by the same person. There are clear connections with the earlier miracle of fishing reported in the synoptic Gospels, also with the two feeding miracles. The symbolism of the story of the meal on the beach became associated with the Eucharist in early Christianity, the fish representing Christ:—*ICTHUS* in Greek, the word for "fish" construed as "Jesus Christ, Son of God and Saviour". Even the number of fish caught assumed symbolic significance representing the universal mission of the Church, as it was believed at the time that there were 153 species of fish. It is a story often portrayed in Christian art. Yet it is also a very down-to-earth story: fishermen addressed by an apparent stranger in the midst of their working life as, "Hey, you guys!"

It is the occasion, however, for a very telling memory, which can only come from the testimony of Peter himself. It is interesting that wherever there is a strand of tradition about Peter in the Gospels, it can often be put into the first person, as here: "He said to me . . . I was hurt." It is very much to the credit of Peter, and a sign of the veracity of the Gospels, that the accounts of his misguided zeal, his weakness and his abject failure were not air-brushed out of the story. His leadership rested upon his forgiveness by Jesus, as this story makes quite clear.

It seems that the threefold questioning of Peter by Jesus in some ways addressed and remedied his threefold denial during the arrest and trial of Jesus: it is about the restoration of a relationship of friendship and trust. In the Greek text, the normal word for love of family and friends alternates with the word that will assume a distinctive Christian character—*agape*—Christ-like love, marked by self-sacrifice and forgiveness. One is rooted in the other, however, as we can see in all the resurrection appearances of Jesus. He was recognized and known among his friends, and it is upon their testimony and loyalty that the historical faith of the Church rests.

What meaning can be given to the threefold question—"Do you love me?" Notice that the love of Jesus always entails love of those who belong to him: there is a connection here with the theme of the Good Shepherd that is apparent in all four Gospels. The question addresses all Christians at all stages of their lives, however, and not just Christian leaders and pastors.

Perhaps the first question, asked with the painful memory of denial still raw, means "Do you really love me?" Like Peter, Christians are challenged by this searching challenge of Jesus. Is he central to our lives, to our thinking and our prayers? Is our loyalty and love towards him the determining direction of our lives? Does he really matter to us, and does our following of him have absolute priority in our lives? It has been well said that if Jesus is not Lord of all our lives, he is not Lord at all.

If this is true, then the second question could be taken to mean "How deeply do you love me?" There comes a moment in any romantic relationship or strong friendship when this is a very pertinent and unavoidable question. So it is in our relationship with Christ. Do we seek him with our whole heart? Do our prayers have a central and regular place in our daily lives? Do we sense his presence when we come to church to worship and receive Holy Communion? Do we expect him to change our lives?

The third question leads on to a very serious challenge indeed. It could mean "How far will you love me?" In the case of Peter, his love of Jesus led to his death in Rome as a martyr. There is an ancient tradition that he was persuaded by the Christian community there to take cover when Nero pounced upon them to make them scapegoats for the devastating fire that he had caused in the city. Surely it would be wise for Peter to lie low in order to continue leading the community in the future? Leaving the city along the Appian Way, Peter encountered Jesus hurrying in the opposite direction. He explained to the Lord what he was doing and then asked Jesus where he was going—*quo vadis*? "To be crucified afresh in the city!" It prompted a change of heart and direction for Peter, and he was crucified upside down and then buried at the edge of the Vatican circus.

This may seem remote and legendary history, but the persecution of Christians today is now at its highest since the worst years of Communism. The UK government has finally woken up to this and commissioned an important report at the prompting of the Church of England and others. Very often it is the poorest communities that are being tyrannized for their Christian belief, either by Islamic fundamentalists in the Middle East and Africa, or by totalitarian regimes like China and North Korea. The forced migration of Christians from the Middle East, where they have lived for centuries, is deplorable but probably now irreversible.

I know from many conversations with Christians who endured persecution in the USSR how important it is that those in free countries know and care about this behaviour and put pressure on barbaric regimes through diplomatic and media channels. There was close collaboration at the time of Communism between the Foreign Office and the churches to good effect. The distorting impact of persecution is a serious cross for people to bear, impacting family as well as church life. What is true for Christians is also true for other religious believers on the receiving end of such treatment. The human right to freedom of worship must be upheld.

To return to Rome. It is very moving and interesting to descend into the depths beneath St Peter's basilica, the Scavi, to explore the necropolis where the body of Peter was initially buried. It is no less moving to be able now to glimpse the casket under the high altar of the wonderful church of St Paul-Outside-the-Walls where Paul's remains still lie. The foundation of the Christian Church thus rests upon the forgiveness and reconciliation of the persecutor—Paul—and the persecuted—Peter. There could be no more powerful demonstration of the truth of the gospel and its ability to change lives and society, and to rebuke for ever the desire to persecute others as contrary to the will of God.

"Do you really love me?" "How deeply do you love me?" "How far will you love me?" These questions of Jesus challenge us all. We are unlikely to be persecuted for our faith. But our prayers can and should reach where we cannot be. Our compassionate intercession for others who are afflicted will enlarge our hearts and enable us to share in the great outpouring of God's love for the world, expressed in the life and death and resurrection of Jesus. It will enable his Spirit "to put love in where love is not".

3 9

Petertide

You are Peter and upon this rock I will build my Church.

I never hear these words (Matthew 16:18) without thinking about their inscription around the inside of the dome of St Peter's basilica in Rome, embodying as they do the theological foundation for the Catholic understanding of the significance of the Papacy. Perhaps the very paradoxical and often scandalous character of that institution and its history gives pause for thought as to the original meaning of our Lord's words. For essentially they constitute a word-play—*Petros/petra*—in Greek, an ironic statement that the Church will comprise people like Simon Peter, who in the end will become rock-like because Christ-like. The memory of Pope Francis delivering such a moving pastoral sermon alone in the middle of the piazza in pouring rain outside St Peter's basilica, on the eve of Holy Week in 2020 and at the height of the first wave of the pandemic in Italy, encapsulates the true heart of the papal pastoral mission for the whole Church.

The first thing to establish on the evidence of the New Testament is that Christ is the Rock on which the Church is built (1 Corinthians 10:4). Those joined to Christ, of which the apostles were the first, become themselves rocks that are also foundations for others, as is evident in the theology of 1 Peter, Ephesians and Revelation (1 Peter 2:4–5; Ephesians 2:20; Revelation 21:14). In the Gospel of Matthew, our Lord commended the person who built his house upon rock, echoing perhaps an earlier parable of the prophet Ezekiel (Matthew 7:24; Ezekiel 13:10–14). In the background, however, there is also the later warning of Jesus himself about being the rock over which some people would stumble (Matthew 21:42–4). To encounter Christ the Rock is to be in a hard and demanding place, which will determine the kind of building that may be constructed upon it, something given and inescapable, not malleable to the human will.

This was certainly the view it would seem of Peter himself in his first letter. He took up the Lord's own use in the Gospels of the paradox of the rejected stone that becomes the cornerstone, to define the Christian vocation as being built upon "a living stone, rejected indeed by men, but with God chosen and precious; as living stones being built up as a spiritual house for a holy priesthood" (1 Peter 2:4–5). A living stone—here is a symbol to conjure with, a great picture of unity built out of diversity. It too contains a hidden warning, however, because stones in a building can develop a life of their own to the detriment of themselves and of those around them. It is possible for stones to weather from within, for fractures to occur that are hidden, but which affect adjacent stones. Often these are invisible from the outside until the stone itself implodes under its own stress and catastrophe ensues. One of the things that vouches for the historical reliability of the Gospels is the fact that Peter never removed from the early Christian tradition, now enshrined in the New Testament, the memory of the fissure that opened up in his own life on the terrible night of the Lord's betrayal and arrest. Instead his own life became a stone remade—by the forging of divine forgiveness and love (John 21:15–19). In Rome, he now lies buried as a martyr, as does Paul—the persecutor and the persecuted, united in their mission and in their Christlike deaths.

A living stone speaks about a process of becoming. Indeed geology provides ample example of what the Fathers meant when they spoke of God's big book—the world of nature—complementing his little book—the Bible. Consider how rocks that are the compression of tiny shells, such as limestone or chalk, are aquifers: so from the bones of the martyrs springs the life of the Church. Or think of sedimentary rocks, sandstone, clay or shale, the product of many years of dull processes, as silt is laid down layer upon layer to be compressed in darkness at the bottom of the sea. What a picture of faithful life and humble discipleship of so many unknown Christians over so many years, sometimes glimpsed in the amazing fossils that occur in such sedimentary beds. Think also of the mineral sources of energy, coal and oil, which contain the energy drawn from the sun by plants millions of years ago. When we read the

Church Fathers and testimonies of the saints, are we not drawing on energy stored in a similar way, though fortunately indestructible? Then there are the igneous rocks, born of great heat and travail, surging up from the inner burning core of the earth, and metamorphosing adjacent rocks to produce gems and precious metals. What a wonderful picture of sanctity, forged by persecution or in the fire of divine love and in the travail of the cross. What a graphic picture geology provides too of the whole manifold composition of the Bible itself. Note also that gold itself, however, has an extra-terrestrial origin.

If we cast our eye across any landscape in England, under its green mantle lie many strata of different rocks and eons of geological history. There are hidden fault-lines and points of collision, of erosion and geomorphology. This is most apparent in a desert: for example, when driving once across the desert of Sinai, the very bones of the earth were evident, mile after mile, the product of terrible forces and upheavals, and almost every form of rock was apparent. Flying across America or Australia three miles up can provide a similar awesome panorama. Is this not a great picture of the life of the Church in history, its composition and conflicts, a dynamic if turbulent process of becoming that is held in the hands of God the Creator? Notice too how so many rocks are created from the remains of something else, so that what appears lost is often remade, sometimes in ways most beautiful and unexpected. The study of history, or the opportunity for ecumenical contact abroad, confirms that this providential process is at work in every part of the Church: for as the Lord says, "Behold, I am making all things new" (Revelation 21:5).

Peter speaks, however, about the creation of a spiritual temple as a deliberate and beautiful building, in which every stone has a specific part to play, structurally and decoratively. This metaphor is best developed by Bede in his book *De Templo*, one of the finest works of ecclesiology produced in the Middle Ages. His theological understanding of how the Church is formed governed the way he recounted the history of the formation of our own church in England. Like Augustine before him writing his *City of God*, Bede sensed the dynamic and creative tension between the Church as it now is, and the Church as it will become. But whereas the process of geology, however purposeful, is inexorable, the process within the Church is a work of divine grace freely accepted by human beings. In the words of Peter, "You are a chosen race, a royal priesthood, a holy nation, a people for God's own possession, that you may show forth the excellency of him who called you out of darkness into his marvellous light" (1 Peter 2:9). These words help to define the secret of Christian vocation (Revelation 2:17).

In Hebrew the two most common words for "rock" convey two different but related meanings: elevation and sharpness. The psalmists make great play on this paradox: "Lead me to the rock that is higher [or too high] for me" (Psalm 61:2). Indeed, for a Christian, almost every reference in the Old Testament to an encounter with rock is susceptible to interpretation with reference to Christ, as Paul intimates—"the rock was Christ" (1 Corinthians 10:4). For the Christian this hard path through the spiritual desert, this narrow and afflicted way (Matthew 7:14), leads to the cross plunged deep into the rock of Calvary, and also to the empty tomb that is carved out of that rock. For as Jesus said: "I, if I be lifted up from [or out of] the earth will draw all people to myself" (John 12:32). In this place, the words of the psalmist come true in a new way. For this place of the rock, Calvary, is the place of breaking and remaking, and of union with him who is the Rock of his people, risen from the empty tomb.

4 0

The Visitation of the Blessed Virgin Mary

2 July

This joyful feast gives a precious glimpse into the wider family of Jesus and indicates the great importance of the support and nurture that was given to him and to his cousin, John, by these faithful Jewish believers. The enthusiasm and kindness of Mary as a young teenage mother-to-be was embraced by the steadfast faithfulness of Elizabeth, whose sensitivity prompted her recognition of the deep significance of what was happening to them both. Thus two sides of such visitation are demonstrated: generous compassion met by receptive sensitivity, bringing the presence of God's Spirit very near.

These principles govern the whole pastoral ministry of the Church in parishes across the country. One of the reasons for a residential ministry is that a priest should visit his or her people, both those who go to church and those who are neighbours. Indeed all residents of a parish are by default members of the Church of England, and in country villages the beneficial impact of this relationship can still be felt. In our benefice, we guarantee a visit within the week of being alerted to some need by churchwardens and others. Obviously funerals require visits as well, and how these are handled is of decisive pastoral priority and importance. They also inspire confidence in the pastoral availability and competence of a local priest.

More generally, the privilege of a parish priest is to be able to spend time with people, with no strings attached and entirely confidentially. Indeed, generous listening in the first instance will often expedite subsequent visits and decisions. The key is to take an encouraging interest in the whole of a person's life. The kitchen table often becomes the weekday altar, as people tell the whole story of their life and of their family. This kind of holistic listening and affirmation is clearly much needed in our society. At funerals, and also at some weddings, a priest is drawn right into the intimate heart of a family. It is certainly a great education in the richness of human nature.

At least once a month, there comes a moment when a priest finds himself or herself in the right place at the right moment, or able to respond immediately to an urgent call to visit someone sick or dying in a home or hospital. This is a great privilege, as a priest is there to support families round tight corners; no home or family is immune from the four "D's": disease, depression, divorce and death. In such situations, the experienced care of someone dispassionate, kind and confidential can be essential and life-giving, both at the time and in the memory long afterwards. By the same token, ineptitude or lack of serious care can leave a real scar in the memory for many years and alienate people from the Church.

In a monastery, visitation is experienced from the other end, as it were. How guests are received is the crucial test of how genuine such a Christian community actually is. As the *Rule of St Benedict* instructs us: "Let guests be received as if they were Christ himself." Many visitors to your community are blessed by how you receive them, by the prayerfulness of Chapel and the kindness of hospitality. This is a place where people encounter God, and it is always a privilege to be part of your life, however briefly. Sensitivity and expectation should therefore govern how guests are received. Patient listening and dispassionate support are something that a monastery can give to any person or their family, often over many years of friendship.

The joyful mystery at the heart of this feast is the fact that within the loving relationship between Mary and Elizabeth the Holy Spirit made his presence felt. The first kick of the child in the womb in response to Mary's arrival not only assured the elderly mother that all was well, it also signified in her mind a moment of prophetic recognition of the significance of Mary's pregnancy. The story certainly puts the focus on the crucial importance of pregnancy and therefore the sanctity of the child in the womb. Clearly Mary felt at home with Elizabeth and as a result the Magnificat poured forth from her soul in a way neither of them ever forgot.

Christian pastoral visitation, given and received, is always part of a continuing dialogue of God's love with people, often through other people who care for them. The lives of individuals and of families can indeed be changed by such generous and sensitive kindness, as a visit or a letter or phone call can be a means of God's grace and presence. The foundation of all Christian visitation is therefore prayer: being open to the call of God through the needs of others and being sensitive to the whole of their reality. We have to pray earnestly that our response will always help and never hinder the loving compassion of God, remembering the words of Jesus, who said that in showing compassion to others we show compassion to him. In the need of the stranger and the afflicted person, Christ himself draws nigh.

This feast also intimates the great ministry of sensitive compassion that has been the hallmark of Mary's continuing ministry in the life of the Church and the world as the mother of God. Our visitations, given and received, are only the humble outskirts of the divine mission of human salvation, in which she continues to support the redemptive work of her Son, our Lord Jesus Christ.

4 1

Transfiguration

The radiance of his glory

The opening lines of the letter to the Hebrews provide a remarkable commentary on the meaning of the transfiguration as recorded in the synoptic Gospels: "God, having of old time spoken to the fathers in the prophets in many parts and in many modes, spoke unto us at the end of these days in his Son, whom he appointed heir of all things, through whom also he made the world." There is therefore both continuity and contrast in the ways in which God revealed himself: in the past, in the Old Testament, it was in various modes and degrees throughout the history of Israel, to the patriarchs first and then to Moses the law-giver, in the Temple and also through the prophets. So in the story of the transfiguration Jesus is seen speaking on a high mountain with Moses and Elijah, their great representatives. He who once appeared to them in the burning bush or in the great turbulence of Sinai now stands in dialogue with them still, their words his words, their testimony his vindication, their message now fulfilled and transformed in his person, who is the living law of God. They were prophets, but Jesus is the Son—the emphasis here is on the nature rather than the personality of the one who now uniquely embodies the fullness of God in human form.

The contrast is clear: in Jesus the whole revelation of God is perfected, prepared for by the long process of tradition which finds its fulfilment in him. His presence at the heart of human history eclipses while affirming the partial revelations that preceded this moment and prepared for it, for they were part of the same light of divine intention and self-communication: in the words of the psalmist, "In thy light shall we see light." So, for example, a lit candle is overtaken when the curtain is drawn and sunlight streams into a room: all that can be seen in place of its light on the wall is perhaps the shadow caused by any smoke, otherwise nothing at all; yet it still burns. In the Gospel story, Jesus was transfigured by divine light shining forth from within him; as Paul said, "the glory of God in the face of Jesus Christ" (2 Corinthians 4:6), "for in him dwells all the fullness of the Godhead bodily" (Colossians 2:9). In the theology of Paul and in this letter to Hebrews also, as in John's Gospel, the transfiguration of Christ brings to completion the creation of the world and of human nature made in the divine image and likeness, as described in the opening chapter of Genesis. In the words of the Nicene Creed, Jesus is truly "Light from Light", for as this letter of Hebrews affirms, he "bears all things [to their perfection and end] by the word of his power".

The moment of transfiguration is something that transcends time and history, however, while constituting its hidden centre. The writer of the letter to Hebrews asserts that it was "at the end of these days" that God spoke to human beings in a Son. This is therefore the messianic *kairos*—the time of divine visitation and presence, of which Jesus himself spoke in the Gospels—the *parousia* now hidden at the heart of the new age of the Church. So in the Gospel story, Jesus promised his disciples: "Truly I tell you: there are some of those standing here who will not taste death before they have seen the kingdom of God come with power" (Mark 9:1). It was "six days later" that Peter, James and John became the new witnesses, on the seventh day—the Sabbath of God—to the moment when Jesus was revealed secretly as the Word of God. For he was and is God speaking with men and women, pitching his tent among them (John 1:14) in fulfilment of the hopes of Israel expressed in the annual Feast of Tabernacles, to which Peter alluded in his initial response to the vision of Jesus flanked by Moses and Elijah. It was from the overshadowing cloud that signifies the divine presence, as in the Exodus story of Sinai, that the voice of the Father acclaimed Jesus: "This is my beloved Son, listen to him." Just as two halves of a nut crack open to reveal the living kernel, so the figures of Moses and Elijah, and all that they represent, now fall away and Jesus is seen alone; the Transfiguration changes things for ever.

The opening of the letter to Hebrews asserts that Jesus as the Son is the creator and the heir, the beginning and the end, the guiding purpose to all existence, "upholding all things by the word of his power". Psalm

2 stands in the background here, as is clear later in the text: "I have set my king upon my holy hill of Zion . . . thou art my Son: this day have I begotten thee." Note that in the opening lines of Hebrews, Jesus is portrayed as the perfect utterance of God, and also as the king, who "sat down on the right hand of the Majesty on high". He is also the priestly redeemer, one of the main themes of this letter, who made purification of sins. In Luke's account of the Transfiguration, Jesus was conversing with Moses and Elijah about the exodus—the deliverance that he was to accomplish in Jerusalem (Luke 9:31). For embedded in the story of the transfiguration is a glimpse of the supreme moment of metamorphosis, when he who emptied himself and took human nature, assuming the form of slave, was obedient even to death on the cross and so was raised up in glory (Philippians 2:6–9). Immediately afterwards in the Gospel account, Jesus commanded his disciples not even to discuss what they had seen until after his resurrection on the eighth day—the new age of God's kingdom. The resurrection and the ascension were the completion of this metamorphosis in Christ of human nature in union with God, the restoration of the damaged image and likeness of God by and in Christ, who alone is the image and likeness of God, the "taking of human nature into God", in the words of the *Quicunque Vult*.

The opening lines of Hebrews then describe Jesus as "being the effulgence of his glory, and the very image [or impress] of his substance". In the words of the nineteenth-century biblical scholar and bishop Brooke Foss Westcott commenting on this passage:

> The first image—*effulgence*—brings out the conception of the source of the Son's being, and of his unbroken connection with the Father, as revealing to man the fullness of His attributes. The second image—*impress* [in Greek *character*]—emphasizes the true personality of the Son, as offering in himself the perfect representation of the divine essence of the Father.

The word "effulgence" can mean either "radiance" or "reflection", but in this passage it is primarily the first meaning, and it conveys the sense of completeness, as in the shining of the sun. In the book of Wisdom, it is used of divine Wisdom itself:

> Like a fine mist she arises from the power of God, a clear effluence
> [or effulgence] from the glory of the Almighty ... she is the
> radiance that streams from everlasting light, the flawless mirror
> of the active power of God, and the image of his goodness.
>
> *Wisdom 7:25-6*

The revealing of God's glory in Jesus fulfilled the hopes and vision of the prophets—for "the glory of the Lord shall be revealed" (Isaiah 40:5). The character of Jesus expressed in a unique human personality the nature and character of God Himself—for as Jesus said, "To have seen me is to have seen the Father" (John 14:9). The writer of Hebrews here uses the word *hypostasis* to express the fullness of God's presence or substance in the person of Jesus—a word that would assume vital significance in later Christian theology of the incarnation and of the Trinity. At this stage, however, its conjunction with the word character gave the sense that the full weight of God's glory and nature was, as it were, impressed as on a coin or seal, on and through the person of Jesus.

When we come to the Eucharist, we ourselves enter into this dynamic pattern of divine revelation: we are taught to hear him who is the Word of God through the Old Testament and the psalms, and in the exposition of his coming in the writings of the New Testament. Then we stand for the Gospel in order, by attentive and prayerful hearing, to glimpse the glory of Jesus Christ the Son of God and so to be changed into his likeness, from glory to glory. In the consecrating prayer, we open our hearts to the shining forth of his glory and presence, through the redemption wrought on the cross, in order to receive the life of the resurrection, "our bread from tomorrow", indicated in the Greek word *epiousisos* used in the Lord's Prayer: "For Thine is the kingdom, the power and the glory of the Father and of the Son and of the Holy Spirit, now and for ever and unto the ages of ages. Amen."

PART 7

The Communion of Saints

4 2

Catherine of Siena

29 April

Catherine of Siena is one of the most significant saints of the European Middle Ages. Born in 1347, she felt the call of our Lord at the age of six as a profound love affair which governed the whole shape of her life thereafter. Despite the reservations of her mother, by 1359 at the age of twelve, she knew her own mind and committed herself to a contemplative life of consecrated virginity, joining the Dominican order as a lay sister in 1362. By the age of twenty, she was active in work among the sick of the city, gathering a small group of disciples and supporters, and beginning a remarkable correspondence of spiritual direction. These *Letters* reached far and wide and drew her into political affairs, as she rebuked clergy for their infidelities and urged the Pope to return from Avignon to Rome.

On 1 April 1375, Catherine received the stigmata in a vision, and this was followed by a number of further costly encounters with our Lord and his holy mother that became the foundation of her spiritual testament, the *Dialogues*. In 1378, she tried to bring peace to the city of Florence at the behest of the Pope, later making her way to Rome where she laboured hard for the unity of the Church. In 1380, aged thirty-three, Catherine had a heart attack and died on 29 April. She is buried in the church of S. Maria sopra Minerva in Rome, the only Gothic church in the city. She was canonized in 1461 and declared a Doctor of the Church by Pope Paul VI in 1970. The outstanding authority and quality of her *Life* is remarkable: it was written by her spiritual director and friend, Raymond of Capua, who became Head of the Dominican Order. What is striking is that her whole spiritual development was accomplished within a very young life and was supported and guided by a coterie of fellow Christians, adept at nurturing the growth of her sanctity.

It is hard to do justice to the wealth of her spiritual legacy, but salient features of it offer inspiration and challenge today. The first is her strong sense of providence, the ability to look on the created world and the vagaries of human life through the loving eyes of God. The Lord placed this challenge before Catherine as a young teenager: "Do you know who you are and who I am? If you know these two things, you will have blessedness within your grasp." He also provided the answer: "You are the one who is not, and I am he who is." This conviction that knowledge of God and of self are inextricably connected became the foundation of her theology. The human person exists only because he or she is loved by God, in whose image and likeness that unique person has been created.

Human beings exist as a result of the overflowing goodness of God, and it is within the stream of this love that they are redeemed from all that mars the divine image within them. Memory, understanding and will are the active components of human consciousness, and these collaborate together in response to communion with God who is within. This communion of intelligent love overflows into love of others, within the love of God and for his sake. In this way, the life of human beings comes to mirror that of the Trinity itself; and belief in the Trinity permeates the prayers and teaching of Catherine. This belief also underlies Catherine's supreme confidence in divine providence: Christ's coming demonstrates the loving mercy of God for fallen humanity. Remade by Christ, human beings may become Christ-like, being always assisted by divine providence.

Catherine was deeply influenced by the memory and example of Francis of Assisi and those who followed him: her life is an embodiment of the spiritual theology of Bonaventura, as well as a faithful following of the teaching of Dominic. Her life was drawn deeply into the reality of Christ crucified, as her biographer relates in careful detail. The Lord set such a fire blazing within her heart that she herself told her confessor that she could not find words to express the divine experiences that she had. On one occasion she sensed that in some mysterious way Christ had removed her own heart and replaced it with his own. Never again could Catherine pray the words: "Lord, I give you my heart." Instead the presence of Christ within her transformed her sense of the reality of his presence in the Eucharist, which became the focus of her spiritual life. Her heart moved in response to the self-giving of Christ in the sacrament, in fulfilment of the words in the psalm: "My heart and my flesh have rejoiced in the Living God." She could testify that "my mind is so full of joy and happiness that I am amazed that my soul stays in my body". This overflowed into her perceptions and love of others.

Catherine's sense of the reality of the presence of Christ in the Eucharist was at times overwhelming. It also underpinned her contemplative intercession for others. Her encounters with Christ laid the basis for her receiving the stigmata while visiting Pisa, an experience that was witnessed by her friends, who saw her body move from being prostrate after receiving Holy Communion to kneeling upright with hands stretched out and light beaming from her face. She confided to her confessor, Raymond of Capua, who had been celebrating the Mass, that she had seen the Lord fixed to the cross coming towards her in a great light. Rays of blood streamed from his wounds to touch her hands and feet and her heart. She prayed that the stigmata would remain invisible, whereupon the rays of blood turned into rays of burning light.

The *Life* of Catherine of Siena is one of the most remarkable testimonies to the spiritual transformation of a young person, and it is corroborated by the profound theology of her *Dialogues*. This in turn is authenticated by the astonishing range of her *Letters*, almost 400 of them, most of which were dictated. What happened in her life was a work of divine grace, nurtured and interpreted within the spiritual life and theology of the Italian Church at the time. She and those who cherished her were conscious of her participation in the communion of saints. The question posed by the life of Catherine to each generation of Christians is simply this: how seriously do we take our own vocation to holiness, individually, as a community, and as a Church?

4 3

Alban the Martyr

22 June

Alban was probably the first saint of these islands of which I became aware when, as a small child, I used to go to St Albans with my mother to visit the elderly couple who had sheltered her during part of the war as an evacuee from London. Exploring the remains of the Roman city and climbing the hill to the great abbey church, with its haunting frescoes and battered shrine, gives to Bede's account in his *History* of Alban's martyrdom a vividness that still resonates in my memory.

In his history of how Christianity came to the English, Bede derived his account from the Gallic church, which treasured the memory of Alban among the martyrs. One of its early bishops, Germanus, visited the shrine in the fifth century. Bede also knew the more fabulous account by the British writer Gildas, but chose to omit it, beyond an interesting mention of others murdered at that time by the Roman authorities; they were Aaron and Julius, who were perhaps Jewish Christian merchants living in Caerleon in South Wales. Bede placed their martyrdom in the time of the emperor Diocletian, but it was probably earlier, perhaps under the emperor Severus early in the third century.

Bede is seldom generous to the British Christians who preceded the church of his own people, the Anglo-Saxons, but he recorded faithfully how miracles still occurred at the shrine of Alban, whose cult had survived the invasion and settlement of his own people: "Here when peaceful Christian times returned, a church of wonderful craftsmanship was built, a fitting memorial of his martyrdom." In the Middle Ages, St Alban's Abbey became a leading and important Benedictine monastery and a great centre of learning, having been refounded by Dunstan during the monastic renewal of the tenth century.

The English Church is unusual in having few martyrs from the early period of its foundation. Indeed it is interesting that Bede and those after him appropriated Alban from this much earlier Roman era. There are four early martyrs of our Church whom we now remember: Alban himself; Boniface, a missionary archbishop, who was murdered in the eighth century in Frisia and is now buried at Fulda in Germany; Edmund, King of East Anglia, murdered by the Vikings in the ninth century and buried at Bury St Edmunds; and Archbishop Alphege of Canterbury, taken hostage and also murdered by the Vikings early in the eleventh century, and buried in the cathedral in Canterbury beside the high altar, where a stone marks the spot today. This paucity of martyrs marks us out from the history of most Continental churches. If we set aside the later martyrs of the Reformation, Protestant and Catholic, and the more controversial figures of Thomas à Becket and King Charles I, we are thin on martyrs, though this is not true of the wider Anglican Communion.

Yet to visit any ancient church in Rome is to be reminded that many of these were founded on the sites of the martyrdom of early Christians. The very shape of a typical Roman basilica embodies this, with its subterranean *confessio* surmounted by the high altar over the place of the burial of the martyr. This is in imitation of the vision in Revelation, where the souls of those slain for the word of God and for the tenacity of their Christian witness lie under the altar of God in heaven (Revelation 6:9). The Greek word *martyr* means "witness". So we must cherish the martyrs who lie under the altar of our own Church in England, remembering that all these four martyrs antedate the Great Schism in the eleventh century between the Eastern and Western churches, and so are revered by Orthodox as well as Catholic and Anglican Christians in our country. In the well-known words of Tertullian, who lived in North Africa in the third century, "The blood of the martyrs is the seed of the Church". Many Christians are still suffering persecution across the world at the present time, and some have been killed as martyrs.

Alban's story is a simple testimony to the power of example. According to Bede's source, he sheltered a fugitive, discovered that he was a Christian priest, and was converted by his example: "When Alban saw this man occupied day and night in continual vigils and prayers, divine grace suddenly shone upon him, and he learned to imitate his guest's faith and devotion." When Roman soldiers came to arrest the priest, Alban went in his stead, disguised in the priest's cloak. It would appear that he was a person of some standing in the Roman city of Verulamium, and his action caused deep embarrassment to the magistrates. They tortured him but failed to break his spirit, so they beheaded him on the hill outside the city, where later his shrine would be built. As Bede said in his *History*, "Its natural beauty suited it as a place now to be made holy by the shed blood of a holy martyr." Death for Alban became the gateway to paradise, marked by a spring of water signifying eternal life.

I noticed also on a recent visit to St Alban's Abbey with my young grandson that a fragment of his relics has now been returned from the church of St Pantaleon in Cologne and placed within the medieval shrine of the saint that stands behind the high altar, as a potent symbol of Christian reconciliation. For me, once standing in the presence of the relics of Alban the martyr in that church in Germany, there was a most personal and moving sense of reconciliation, fulfilling the prophetic words of the Christian poet Venantius Fortunatus, cited by Bede at the beginning of his account: "*Albanum egregium fecunda Britannia profert*— Noble Alban, fertile Britain's son". As we commemorate Alban, let us remember before God all our fellow Christians across the world who are enduring persecution for their faith at the present time.

4 4

Bonaventure

15 July

Bonaventure was born around the year 1217 in Bagnoregio, which is near Orvieto in Italy. He was educated at the University of Paris, where he also taught alongside his friend, Thomas Aquinas, for some years until 1257 when he was made Minister General of the Franciscans. This engaged him in a relentless labour of organizing, teaching and preaching, travelling on foot across the length and breadth of Europe to supervise the growing Franciscan movement. His commitment to this vocation prevented him from accepting the post of Archbishop of York in 1265, but in 1273 he was commanded by Pope Gregory X to become a cardinal and bishop. Bonaventure joined the pope at the second Council of Lyons, where he died on 15 July 1274.

As the leader of the Franciscans during a difficult period in their history, Bonaventure was regarded by many as virtually the second founder of the movement. Certainly all that he taught and wrote was intended to put the memory and legacy of Francis of Assisi on a firm biblical and doctrinal footing. Bonaventure was also concerned to raise the standard of learning and preaching among the Franciscans, in order to advance the mission of the gospel and also to protect the growing movement from criticism. He brought all his expertise and experience as an academic teacher of theology in Paris to bear upon the formation and nurture of those now in his pastoral care.

Bonaventure was unusual in that his mind was both sharply analytical and eloquently poetic. He also had a formidable memory, especially of scripture, and there is nothing that he teaches that is not rooted in the Bible. He distilled the wisdom of many who had gone before him, both his immediate mentors in Paris, and the great teachers of the Western Church, beginning with Augustine, whose theology was the paramount influence on Bonaventure's own. Many rich strands of teaching flow like tributaries into Bonaventure's thought, notably that of Gregory the Great, Anselm, Bernard of Clairvaux, and also the writings of the fifth-century Syrian theologian Dionysius, recently translated afresh into Latin, which exercised a distinctive influence on how Bonaventure structured his thought. To some extent, therefore, he was conveying the wealth of this spiritual tradition to his Franciscan hearers, but at the same time, he was transposing and transforming it. Bonaventure was in every way a brilliant communicator, and this is most evident in the many sermons that he composed and circulated as models for use in Franciscan preaching and ministry, and also in his masterly and extensive *Commentary on St Luke's Gospel.*

Bonaventure is the most consistently Christ-centred of theologians, and the spiritual goal of Christian theology is never out of his sight. He did not regard the study of theology as an end in itself, let alone a simply academic exercise; nor did he consider it on a par with philosophy. He believed instead what Irenaeus of Lyons had actually declared many centuries before him in the second century: that the vision of God is the life of a person, and the glory of God is the living human being. Christian theology is concerned with the redemption and transformation of human nature by the Spirit of Christ, who became man so that human beings might become divine in him.

Bonaventure is rightly regarded as a supreme mystical theologian, in the sense that he believed and taught that experience of the transforming love of Christ is at the heart of all Christian thought and prayer. This love constrains a person, as it did in the case of Francis and Clare of Assisi, to the point of their participating spiritually in the redeeming suffering of the crucified Christ. Then the glory of God descends to transfigure a person, deifying him or her, and revealing that the soul is indeed made in the image and likeness of God and has a profound affinity with him. Bonaventure believed strongly that human beings are called to become by grace partakers of the divine nature in union with Christ.

Bonaventure took to heart and taught assiduously that, in the words of Augustine, God has made us for himself, and our hearts are empty and restless until they find their rest in him. The loving call of Christ is to enable a willing return to God, and this is the meaning of Christian life, thought and prayer; for Bonaventure, love always transcended learning. It is the work of reason to come to understand Christ, who is the truth, by faith as well as by thought, and so to come to perceive more deeply what is revealed by divine revelation in the Bible and mediated through the sacraments of the Church.

Bonaventure had a very positive expectation of what could be accomplished by the Holy Spirit in human nature. He himself embodied the truth that he taught, being very well loved as an outstanding Christian in his own lifetime and thereafter. He insisted that wisdom and contemplation have to be motivated by a burning desire for God, for his goodness and his love. This desire must order all other desires, and it must not be distracted by false values, moral, intellectual or spiritual.

Human beings are designed to be able, by the grace of the Spirit of Christ and through faith, reason and love, to apprehend the ground of truth in God, and also the meaning of reality as they experience it within the life of the Church that is set in the midst of human history. In Christ the end or goal of history is revealed to be in its midst and at its heart, at the cross of Calvary, but it is also within the human heart as the hidden place of divine encounter and spiritual ascent. All these mysteries and possibilities spring from the self-giving and revealing of God that is expressed in creation and scripture, and whose meaning and power are revealed in the incarnation, the cross and the resurrection of Christ. Herein is the measure of human redemption and sanctification by the indwelling of the Holy Spirit, and also the revealing of its eternal destiny.

For Bonaventure, the example of Mary the mother of the Lord always pointed the way. On the authority of Jesus himself. Bonaventure believed that Mary's humble and loving response to the call of God remains for all Christians the secret to the purpose and proper ordering of each human life: "Behold, I am the handmaid of the Lord: may it be to me according to your word."

4 5

Mary Magdalene

22 July

"My song shall be of mercy and judgement" (Psalm 101:1). These lovely words from the psalms encapsulate the message of this Gospel reading (Luke 7:36–50), while the surest guide among the Fathers to the meaning and significance of this moving story is Gregory the Great in his Gospel homily about this passage. Gregory's approach was deeply pastoral, perceptive and sensitive: he noted how Christ drew the woman inwardly by his mercy, and received her outwardly by his gentleness. We see the truth of this also in the encounter of Jesus with a young woman taken in the act of adultery and thrust into his presence in the Temple (John 8:1–11). In the end, both these women were enabled to serve God once again by their repentance, as completely as they had earlier rejected his law by their sins.

Commenting on Luke's story, which is unique to this Gospel, Gregory contrasted the awareness in the woman of the extent of her sinfulness with the blindness of the Pharisee, who "criticized the sick woman on account of her moral failings, but was himself ill from the wound of self-esteem, thus condemning in his heart the true doctor, Jesus, who welcomed and accepted her". Jesus thus found himself between two spiritually sick people. Worse still, the Pharisee believed that Jesus was being defiled by the other person's sins, because her compunction did not touch his heart. In her loving devotion the woman set an example of deep compassion of heart, suffering inner compunction in such a way that her generous hands and tears gave evidence of her inner sorrow and repentance.

This story is a good example of the principle Gregory enunciated elsewhere that the more spiritual a miracle is the more sure it is. For Luke has given here an insight into the inner psychological and spiritual drama often hidden within the simpler outlines of other Gospel miracles of compassion. Gregory's verdict was eloquent:

> She completely burned away the corrosion of her sins because she became greatly enkindled by the fire of love. The more the heart of a sinner is consumed by the fire of love, the more fully the damage of sin is consumed.

This story is also an example of why people mocked Jesus as "a glutton and a drinker, a friend of tax-collectors and sinners!" (Luke 7:34). The figure of the fallen woman is a well-known one in every society: someone to be used and then despised, to be blamed for the sins of those with whom she has committed immorality. In a male-dominated society such as the one in which Jesus lived, she was a powerful scapegoat, and this can still be true today.

In the Old Testament, however, such a woman was also a symbol of Israel, a figure of unfaithfulness used by several of the prophets. According to Hosea, God persists in his love for Israel in all her unfaithfulness. The heart of the prophet's message lies in these words that shed light also on this encounter in the Gospel: "Come, let us return to the Lord, for he has torn us, but he will heal us; he has wounded us, but he will bind up our wounds" (Hosea 6:1). For God says, "I shall heal my people's unfaithfulness and I shall love them freely" (Hosea 14:4).

This Gospel story also parallels the famous parable told by Jesus of the prodigal son, with its challenge to the elder brother who, while physically near and apparently loyal to his father, was in fact very far from him in his heart (Luke 15:11–32). This is a true story of a prodigal daughter, a notorious local sinner, excluded from the religious life of her people as a sin-bearer. Jesus was not afraid to be "reckoned among the transgressors" (Isaiah 53:12), however, and he was not afraid of guilt by association, even though being touched by such a woman rendered him ritually unclean as a rabbi.

This is also a story about friendship restored, in contrast to pretended hospitality: "You gave me no kiss of friendship and welcome; but she has been kissing my feet ever since I came in." A sincere kiss of peace rapidly became the hallmark of Christian fellowship. It embraced Jew and Greek, slave and freeman, male and female gathered round the common meal of the Eucharist (Galatians 3:28). Yet tragically the word used here to speak of the woman's lavishing of kisses upon the feet of Jesus is also used to describe Judas' act of betrayal in the garden of Gethsemane. For running through this story is an act of social betrayal, set in the midst of apparent hospitality. The Pharisee had invited Jesus out of curiosity, and his approach was disdainful, negligent and snobbish. His attitude became apparent in his inner thoughts, which Jesus knew only too well: "If this man were a real prophet, he would know who this woman is who is touching him up, and what a bad character she is." The Pharisee sees only a sinful woman, a mere nobody, and he sneers at her. Jesus, however, had already encountered her, it would seem, and has begun to change her life. The host meanwhile neglected his guest, failing in the most obvious duties of courtesy and hospitality. Jesus was not really welcome, and perhaps such painful personal experiences lay behind some of his most famous parables.

Suddenly, however, the Pharisee becomes a named person—Simon: how and why? Is this in fact his story also, his moment of recognition, compunction and repentance? Did both these very different people find their way into the earliest Christian Church? The directness of how the challenge of Jesus was remembered may reflect the way in which his words were seared into Simon's memory and conscience. Note, however, that Jesus had first to appeal to Simon's pocket in order to make him see sense. Simon understood the psychology of money better than the hearts of other men and women, as was true long before when the prophet Nathan challenged King David over his adultery (2 Samuel 12). This sharp encounter is an acted-out parable about forgiveness that Jesus expanded upon in another context (Matthew 18:21–35). Being let off a debt is a poor metaphor, however, for experiencing the forgiveness of sins that alone can renew a person. Jesus challenged Simon with these devastating questions: "Do you see this woman? Do you actually see her as a real human person?" For the inner betrayal of sin breeds a blindness of attitude that too often blames and depersonalizes, and so often paves the way for active or passive cruelty, abuse and neglect.

By contrast the woman crouching at the feet of Jesus behind the couch on which he was reclining at table becomes a figure of grace and graciousness. Her tears, her tender care and her generosity demonstrate the central truth of the gospel, for as Jesus observed, "Her great love proves that her many sins have been forgiven; for where little has been forgiven, little love is shown." These are words of mercy and judgement. Her tears were those of a heart broken by compunction and renewed in its tenderness by divine love. The liberating power of Jesus was expressed in his command to her, in the hearing of all those who would still condemn her: "Your sins are forgiven . . . your faith has saved you . . . now go in peace." These reassuring words contain Luke's Gospel message in a nutshell.

Tradition associated this story with Mary Magdalene, who is mentioned immediately afterwards in this Gospel (Luke 8:2). If so, the truth that such love is stronger than death was certainly demonstrated by the story of her lingering and weeping in the garden of the resurrection (John 20:11). There Jesus truly saw Mary as the person whom he loved and who loved him, addressing her personally as "Mary". She was embraced eternally, if not immediately physically, by the One whose love for her, and for each human person, is indeed stronger than death. In the lovely words of the Song of Songs, which is in so many ways a commentary on what is happening in these two Gospel stories: "Many waters cannot quench love, neither can the floods drown it" (Song of Songs 8:7).

4 6

Clare of Assisi

11 August

What was the spiritual life and significance of Clare, who died enclosed within her monastery of St Damian in Assisi on this day in 1253? Within less than two years, she was canonized by Pope Alexander IV, who had always been such a stalwart support and guide to her and to those following in the footsteps of Francis of Assisi. Clare herself had received her vocation and tonsure from Francis, whom she cherished while he yet lived, and whose memory and teaching she kept alive by her own example and that of her community of nuns until her own death. From the moment of her enclosure, Clare never left her monastery, living a life of great austerity, simplicity and radical poverty that was finally endorsed by Pope Innocent IV personally in 1253 just days before her death.

We catch a glimpse of her hidden life in Christ and its significance from a letter of Bonaventure, written from La Verna in 1259 to Clare's sisters in Assisi, when he was Minister General of the Franciscan Order:

> May you never wish to have anything else under heaven except what your Mother taught you, namely Jesus Christ crucified. After her example, hasten, dear daughters, after the fragrance of His blood. Boldly take hold of the mirror of poverty, the path of humility, the shield of endurance, and the badge of obedience. Then, enkindled by the fire of divine love, give your heart totally to Jesus, who on the cross offered Himself to God the Father for us.

It is worth reflecting that Bonaventure wrote this letter during his retreat on La Verna, an experience that changed his life and deepened his spiritual vision as the guardian of the Franciscans. The first fruit of this experience is enshrined in his *Journey of the Mind to God* that was composed in 1259. The living example of the sisters formed by Clare proved to be a foundation for Bonaventure's subsequent spiritual writing. His *Life of St Francis* was a distillation of his own conviction about the spiritual significance of the Christ-like Francis, which became the inspiration of his theological teaching. Moreover, just as Mary, the mother of the Lord, may be glimpsed in the wings of the Gospel story, so Clare peeps out to us in relation to Francis in the select body of writings that remains from her hand, as well as in the potent spiritual tradition of the Poor Clares to this day. Bonaventure was present at the dedication of the church that still contains Clare's body in Assisi.

The most important of these writings are her four letters to Agnes of Prague, a royal princess who followed the example of Clare in 1234 and founded a small Franciscan church, nunnery and hospital in that city. She remained a nun there for fifty-four years and died in 1282. It is within these pastoral letters of spiritual direction and encouragement that we may hear Clare's quiet voice directly, sometimes drawing on texts from the Bible and the liturgy of the Church to express her meaning. Clare described Agnes as "the spouse, the mother and the sister" of Christ, who was "adorned with the sign of true virginity and most holy poverty". She bade her to "be strengthened in the holy service she had undertaken out of an ardent desire for Jesus, the Poor Crucified One". We come close to the heart of Clare's own vocation in her words to Agnes.

To her sisters in Assisi, Clare proved a true spiritual mother, as these final words from her blessing to them reveal: "I bless you in my life and after my death as much as I can and even more than I can, with all the blessings with which the Father of mercies has and will always bless His own sons and daughters in heaven and on earth." We also seek her blessing and her intercession on this, the glad day of her passing.

4 7

The Blessed Virgin Mary

15 August and 8 September

The poignant words in John 19:25–7 should anchor our thinking about Mary, the mother of the Lord, in the stark reality of her humanity. No mother should ever have to witness the torture and murder of her own child, yet across the world, this is happening today; in some places it is our fellow Christians who are the victims of such barbarity. It is no service to the memory of Mary to relegate her to a stained-glass window or to put her on a pedestal as a statue. Instead, we should see her as the key witness to the mystery of our Lord's incarnation, Passion and resurrection.

Today's Gospel story is unique to the Gospel of John and it has inspired some of the greatest Christian art, poetry and music, notably the *Stabat Mater*: "Standing near the cross of Jesus was his mother." These terrible words bear eloquent witness to a mother's faithfulness, courage and determination. Yet Mary does not stand alone. With her are two other named witnesses: her sister Mary and also Mary Magdalene, both later witnesses to the resurrection. If Clopas the husband of Mary is actually Cleopas in the last chapter of Luke's Gospel, then we have the striking fact that Luke's Gospel begins and ends with private family memories of Jesus of a very intimate kind. Behind these stands the quiet authority of Mary, who appears to have remained in Jerusalem until at least the day of Pentecost. It was her memory also that testified to the story of the annunciation, the birth in Bethlehem, the coming of the shepherds, and the presentation in the Temple of the child Jesus. On that occasion, she received the grim prediction that a sword would pierce her own heart too, words fulfilled as she stood near the cross of her son.

The influence of the mother of the Lord may perhaps also be discerned in the spirit of the teaching of Jesus, his profound empathy and ability to communicate mercy and compassion. There is in a way a feminine spirit to the Beatitudes and to some of the Lord's parables. His capacity to relate to women so openly may also have sprung from his upbringing at home. Certainly every time we use his prayer, "Our Father", we remember that his word for Father was "Abba", the term he would have used for Joseph as his father while he was still alive.

The Greek word for "witness" is *martyr*. In the example of Mary, we may see how witnessing and suffering are entwined together in Christianity. She suffered the social opprobrium of having started her pregnancy before marriage, in a society where a girl could be killed for such misconduct. She endured being uprooted during her pregnancy, giving birth in cramped conditions, fleeing as a refugee to Egypt, and returning home to Nazareth, where not everyone accepted Jesus, and on one occasion they tried to lynch him. She had to endure pressure from her wider family, perhaps after the death of her husband Joseph, to rein Jesus in. She accompanied him on his final journey to Jerusalem and witnessed his death. Notice that in the Gospel today, Jesus commended her to the one male disciple who was still standing by, traditionally John. Early Christian tradition tells of her life in his home, initially in Jerusalem and later at Ephesus.

Mary is also seen as the mother of the Church by virtue of her prayers and compassionate intervention. Across the Catholic and Orthodox world, also in Syria, Egypt, Ethiopia and other ancient centres of Christianity, Mary is highly venerated as the human link with her son, and as a loving collaborator in his ministry of healing and compassion. It is lamentable that at the Reformation, this sense of Mary's continuing ministry in the Church was abandoned in England, where for centuries she had been highly regarded. But the witness of so many Christians across the ages and across the world today cannot be ignored. Mary stands as the great and merciful intercessor, a loving link between Jesus and ourselves: "Holy Mary, pray for us sinners, now and in the hour of our death."

Mary is also mother of and among the saints, the first and most pre-eminent Christian saint by virtue of her close union with Jesus her son, a union that was biological but also spiritual, as confirmed in the words of Jesus: "Blessed are those who hear the word of God and keep it." This is not to romanticize Mary or to turn her into a cult figure, which actually distances the impact of her witness. Instead we should take to heart her words at the annunciation: "Behold, I am the servant of the Lord: may it be unto me according to your word." This lies at the heart of her vocation and example to us all and in three particular ways.

Firstly, at the heart of our prayer we should make her words our own. We are called to welcome Christ into the very heart of our life, so that in the words of Paul, Christ may be formed in us. "Behold, I am the servant of the Lord: may it be unto me according to your word." We may ask her to pray with us that this may be so, that we may truly cherish her son and that he may be born within us spiritually.

Secondly, when we come to receive the consecrated bread of Holy Communion, that tiny wafer, we should use her words again: "Behold, I am the servant of the Lord: may it be unto me according to your word." What are the Lord's words to us at Communion? "This is my body that is offered up and broken for you." This tiny thing becomes the living loving bond between ourselves and Christ who is truly the Bread of Life.

Thirdly, you would not drop the wafer in Holy Communion, nor would you drop a baby. Mary's example shows us how her care of Jesus, through pregnancy and childbirth, raising and loving him, supporting his ministry, and witnessing his suffering and death, demonstrates the true measure of Christian dedication in marriage and parenthood: "for better, for worse; for richer, for poorer; in sickness and in health, until death us do part". The commitment of marriage is thus the commitment of parenthood too, for this faithful and self-sacrificial love is what all children need, what we all need, as it is the only sure foundation and security we can offer to others.

Mary is called mother of God in the precise sense that she offered to Jesus her son a unique mother's love, a human mother's love. The astonishing thing is that God stooped to receive such a love in this way, and without it the incarnation of Jesus as God's Son could never have occurred as it did. Thus every action of care for a child has become a sacramental sharing in the creating love of God, who brings into being from nothing human persons made in his image and likeness, whom he seeks to redeem and to restore in the likeness of Christ himself. This is what we commit ourselves to when we pray in the words of Mary: "Behold, I am the servant of the Lord: may it be unto me according to your word."

4 8

Aidan of Lindisfarne

31 August

The feast of Aidan falls on 31 August, and he died in 651. He was the Irish missionary bishop sent from the monastery founded by Columba on the island of Iona at the request of King Oswald of Northumbria, who had become a Christian while in exile there. We only know about Aidan from book three of Bede's *History* of how Christianity came to the English. Bede grew up in the area of Northumbria and was particularly influenced by the work of the Irish missionaries who accompanied and succeeded Aidan. He had close friendships with the monastic community on the tidal island of Lindisfarne, which Aidan had founded as his base. Bede's sympathy for them and his appreciation of their spiritual significance enabled him to paint a vivid, authentic and attractive picture of Aidan as an outstanding missionary monk and bishop. Aidan died in his private chapel that stood where Bamburgh parish church now stands, and the church there is dedicated to his memory.

The first Irish missionary sent from Iona in 635 after Oswald secured his kingdom was rather a disaster and returned home frustrated with his barbarian flock! So Aidan was sent instead, because "he was pre-eminently endowed with the grace of discretion". In fact, he relied initially on the king himself to act as his interpreter while he learnt the language of his hearers. The king gave him the tidal island of Lindisfarne as his base because it was relatively secure, in sight of the royal fortress at Bamburgh and easily accessible by sea. The present monastic ruins date from the early Norman period when the monastery was revived by the monks of Durham. It had been sacked repeatedly by the Vikings, beginning in 793, and its community was forced to migrate with the relics of Cuthbert until they finally settled at Durham where the cathedral now stands.

Aidan taught by example; as Bede said: "He taught no other way of life than that which he himself practised among them." He refused possessions and always travelled on foot. He was fearless towards the rich, using their gifts to him as alms for the poor or to redeem slaves, some of whom he trained for the priesthood. It is Bede who ensured that the memory of Aidan as the founder of the monastery of Lindisfarne was upheld and appreciated, and not eclipsed by the growing cult of Cuthbert. Their inner spiritual life, both Aidan's and Cuthbert's, was wrought during solitary vigils upon the Inner Farne Island, which lies in sight of both Lindisfarne and Bamburgh. Their compassion and effectiveness as missionaries and pastors flowed from their costly spiritual struggle as ascetic and contemplative Christians.

For Bede, Aidan became the yardstick by which every other bishop mentioned in his *History* was to be measured:

> Such was his love of peace and charity, temperance and humility that his soul triumphed over anger and greed, and at the same time he despised pride and vanity. His diligence in carrying out and teaching the commandments of God, and his diligence in studying and keeping vigil at night proved to be the foundation of his moral authority as priest and bishop. He did not hesitate to rebuke the proud and overbearing, and in kindly tenderness comforted the weak in society, while helping and championing the poor.

In Bede's mind, the ministry of Aidan was truly apostolic as from "a person of outstanding gentleness, devotion and moderation". His portrait of Aidan probably tells us a great deal about the character of Bede himself.

Bede tells two memorable stories about Aidan. In the first, he was sitting at an Easter feast with King Oswald when the steward announced that a crowd of desperately poor folk were at the door of the king's hall. Without hesitation Oswald commanded that a fine silver plate being used for the feast should be broken up into small pieces and given to the poor there and then. Aidan was so moved by this generosity that he grasped the king's hand and declared "May this hand never decay!" Long after Oswald died in battle against a pagan king, his hand was treasured incorrupt in the royal chapel at Bamburgh, as a relic of his sanctity and also of his death as a martyr fighting to defend his Christian kingdom.

The other story reveals the influence that Aidan had over Oswald's successor, King Oswine. The young king offered the elderly bishop a fine horse so that he could travel around and ford rivers more safely. It came with an elaborate harness and its equivalent today would be an expensive car. Aidan was reluctant to ride, however, and while on a journey he encountered a poor man to whom he promptly gave away the king's horse. At supper, the king gently challenged the bishop and said that surely there were plenty of humbler beasts that could have been offered instead. Aidan's reply was tart: "Surely this son of a mare is not more precious to you than that child of God?" A little later, as the king stood in front of the fire with his companions, these words hit home. He threw down his sword, knelt at Aidan's feet, and told him that he could do as he wished with their treasure. Aidan was deeply moved—but troubled also, saying privately in Irish that "I know that this king will not live long, for I never saw a more humble king". Oswine was indeed murdered and Aidan died twelve days afterwards. How could a king be a true Christian when he had first and foremost to be an effective war leader?

This simple and ascetic bishop proved a stay and prop to the fragile political order in Northumbria which had made his mission a possibility. Even as a critic he was a true servant and friend, standing for the values of an eternal king as a monk who had died to the world. Aidan thus embodied the authority of Christ, who came "not to be served but to serve". His vocation and ministry called forth that vision also from those two kings, Oswald and Oswine, in different but memorable ways. Theirs was an alliance with Aidan built upon genuine friendship and respect. His evangelism proceeded by example and education and without any coercion, for underpinning it was a sacrificial monastic way of life which was no sham. This enabled Aidan, and all those who followed his example, to relate to and to evangelize all manner of folk, high and low. In many ways the figure of Aidan is an important key to unlocking the theological and moral purpose of Bede's writing of his *History*. Aidan's memory remains alive today on the holy island of Lindisfarne in its parish church and in its retreat centre, both of which stand under the shadow of the haunting and beautiful ruins of the later monastery that was recreated there in the Norman period and which lasted until the Reformation.

4 9

Gregory the Great

3 September

"Non Angli sed Angeli."

The importance and significance of Pope Gregory the Great, whose feast day falls on 3 September, cannot be in any doubt; and his memory remains a focal point of unity for all Catholic and Anglican Christians, in this country and across the world. The monastery that he founded in Rome on the Caelian hill, San Gregorio al Celio, remains today in the hands of the Camaldolese Benedictines as a great centre of biblical and spiritual teaching. In the corner of its lovely early Baroque church can be found the site of Gregory's own cell, still furnished by a marble chair from his household. He died in 604, having served as pope for thirteen turbulent years. He defined his papal ministry as being "the servant of the servants of Christ", a title which still remains in use by the papacy, and which sums up the pastoral and spiritual legacy of Gregory the Great.

For English Christians, Gregory remains pre-eminently our apostle, the pope who sent Augustine from Rome to Canterbury in 597 to create the Church in England that remains to this day, with an unbroken succession of more than one hundred Archbishops of Canterbury. The story of this mission is told principally in the pages of Bede's *History* as a result of his research into the documents that remained in Canterbury and in Rome recounting what happened. But there is another line of transmission in the form of an anonymous *Life* of Gregory that was written at Whitby, perhaps by a nun there, before Bede wrote his *History*. It is striking that the first two hagiographies of Gregory should have been composed in England long before he was formally commemorated in such a way in Rome itself.

Both historical traditions speak about a moment of personal vision that impelled Gregory to act in the way that he did. Walking through the slave market in the Forum that was hard by his family home, Gregory saw some fair-haired young people on sale. Asking where they came from, he was told that they came from "Anguli", the land of the Angles, from the very edge of the known world. Hence Gregory's famous pun—"*non Angli sed Angeli!*"—"Not Angles but Angels!" It seems that Gregory wanted to leave Rome and lead the mission himself, but it was not to be. Instead, when he became pope, he took steps to prepare for such an unusual initiative. The evidence is found in his many letters, which also give us a vivid picture of the many demands placed upon him at the time; some of these letters were included by Bede in his *History*.

Because of the way that Bede told the story in his *History*, the memory of Gregory and the example of his teaching as a monk and theologian deeply influenced the character of the English Church, founded as it was upon monastic mission and education rather than coercion. When English missionaries and scholars like Boniface and Alcuin went to work on the Continent, they imbued the Frankish and German churches with the teaching of Gregory the Great. This was because of the singular combination of influences that formed Gregory's approach to being pope, which find expression in his most important writings.

First and foremost, he compiled the only handbook that exists on the way in which Christian pastoral authority should be exercised, called the *Pastoral Rule*. It addresses practical ways in which a Christian pastor has to understand the temperaments of those under his or her care, their strengths and weaknesses. Such was its versatility and practicality that it proved relevant not only to running a diocese or monastery, but also in running schools. Gregory placed education at the heart of mission in a way that has determined the character of English Christianity ever since. The *Pastoral Rule* was also of use to later Christian rulers, influencing the whole way in which the idea of Christian kingship developed in the centuries after Gregory's death. It was one of the books that King Alfred the Great had translated into English at the end of the ninth century.

Closely connected to this pastoral legacy was the way in which Gregory wrote up the life of the early Italian saints, most notably that of Benedict, whose monastic *Rule* Gregory commended. His *Life of Benedict* is probably one of the most influential biographies of a saint ever written, a fitting companion to the no less influential *Rule of St Benedict*. It was Gregory who demonstrated that a bishop could be, and ideally should be, a monk living in a community. The monastic bishop became a feature of Anglo-Saxon Christianity in great figures like Dunstan, Ethelwold and Oswald in the tenth century.

Gregory succeeded in the distilling of Western Patristic theology, principally drawn from the writings of Augustine, and its presentation in pastoral and moral terms of immediate practicality and relevance. His Gospel homilies, his commentaries on Ezekiel and on the book of Job, built a bridge between theology and Christian life, between belief and morality. Central to this enterprise was the role of preaching, and fundamental to it was the life of prayer. Gregory's own example and his frankness about the rigours of the spiritual life gave a language of expression to the spirituality of the early Middle Ages. For Gregory, the Christian spiritual life is a prolonged education and discipline—and there are no shortcuts.

This was the inner miracle of Gregory's life and also of the mission to the English which he inspired and guided. His teaching and example influenced the missionaries in their approach to political authority, their investment in education, and in their expectations of sanctity. As the Whitby biographer observed, the manifold work of the Holy Spirit is apparent "in the healing of souls, as our own Gregory has explained, because it is in them that we are restored to the image of God".

5 0

Holy Cross Day

14 September

The dedication of a processional cross at Marlborough College

"Far be it from me to glory, save in the cross of our Lord Jesus Christ, through which the world has been crucified unto me, and I unto the world" (Galatians 6:14). These are some of the earliest written words in the New Testament and also some of the most personal, coming as they do at the very end of Paul's letter to the Galatians, which is one of his earliest letters, and in the part which he wrote with his own hand. How can the cross, a symbol of cruelty, shame and degradation, of God's curse, become a symbol of glory and a means of God's grace? Paul had no illusions about this paradox at the heart of Christianity, because a crucified Messiah was a contradiction in terms: the Messiah was God's chosen one, so how could he become God's cursed one? Yet Paul affirmed to the Corinthian church that "we preach a crucified Messiah, to Jews a scandal, and to Greeks sheer lunacy". He was sure that at the cross, "God was in Christ reconciling the world unto himself: . . . for him who knew no sin, God made to be sin on our behalf; that we might become the righteousness of God in him." The cross is the place where God intervened decisively in human existence: it is the place of judgement—but also of life.

> The royal banners forward go:
>> the cross shines forth in mystic glow;
> Where he in flesh, our flesh who made;
>> our sentence bore, our ransom paid.

These haunting words of the sixth-century Latin poet, Venantius Fortunatus, from his hymn *Vexilla Regis*, lead us into the mystery of the cross. This is a processional hymn, as the cross comes into view leading the banners of the Church, the earthly citadel of the kingdom of God. From the heart of the cross shines forth the hidden glory of God to which the resplendence of silver and gold can bear witness. For on the cross hung crucified, in all the vulnerability of human flesh, God the Creator, who stooped to become in our flesh the re-creator of the fragile human beings that he had made. In Christ, he emptied himself of his power, to become suspended helpless on this bitterest yoke that racked him to death, "obedient even unto death on a cross".

When we process into church or out of church, with the cross leading the way, we follow and we stand with God in his hour of grieving, in words whose truth Dietrich Bonhoeffer discovered in the depths of a Gestapo prison in 1944. But we also celebrate the fact that this is an empty cross, the symbol of the resurrection, of Christ's trampling down death by death, of the great hope of new and eternal life for human beings made in the image and likeness of God. "For this light shines on in the darkness, a darkness which has neither understood it nor put it out."

How can this be? In John's Gospel, Jesus pointed his learned visitor, Nicodemus the Pharisee, back to the strange story in our first reading: "As Moses lifted up the serpent in the wilderness, even so must the Son of Man be lifted up: that whoever believes in him, may in him have eternal life." Later, in the last week of his life, Jesus proclaimed to those around him: "I, if I be lifted up from out of the earth, will draw everyone unto myself." In the ancient tradition of the Exodus story, it was the people's rebellion that laid them open to that which would destroy them: it is another version of the story of the fall of Adam and Eve in the garden of Eden. Moses, the leader whom they spurned for a time, became their intercessor, making peace with God on their behalf. The bronze serpent became a sign of God's forgiveness and healing: if people would only look upon it, they might live again, free from their pain. Did they all look, however? By a strange and tragic irony, many years later, this very symbol of life became an idol to which the people burnt incense, and as such it was destroyed at a time of reformation in Israel.

So the symbol of the cross is an ambiguous and challenging one. It forces us to confront that which leads to our own destruction: our willingness to crucify others, by thought, word and deed. It is a symbol of the ultimate betrayal that will force upon another human being a degrading and lingering death, not just physical, but also social and psychological. It stands as the absolute condemnation of capital punishment and torture, in every place and at any time. Yet in venerating the cross we can easily turn it into an empty symbol, devoid of meaning, or worse still an idol, shielding ourselves from its painful truth. This has happened in history: and at the Reformation, or during the French and Bolshevik revolutions, many crosses were viciously destroyed as a result.

The cross before us in church reminds us too of that which is laid upon us as Christians, called indeed to stand with God in his hour of grieving at so much that is corrupt and evil in our day. For as Jesus said to his disciples, "If anyone would come after me, let him deny himself, and take up his cross, and follow me." . . . "For how narrow is the gate and afflicted the way that leads to life, and how few be they who find it!" What does it mean to bear the cross of Christ, or as Paul described it, "to be crucified to the world"? In the words of a recent spiritual writer, it means "standing—holding things without being deflected by your own desires or the desires of other people round you. Then things work out through patience. How things alter we do not know, but the situation alters." In short, it means bearing the inner hurt that people often project upon us, in the spirit of Jesus, who taught and demonstrated love even of enemies: "Father, forgive them for they do not know what they are doing."

The mystery of the cross is how the tree of death, encircled by evil and human spite, becomes the tree of life. We hear again the poetry of Venantius Fortunatus, in his other hymn celebrating the cross—*Pange lingua gloriosi*:

> Faithful Cross, above all other,
> one and only noble Tree,
> None in foliage, none in blossom;
> none in fruit thy peer may be.

In many ways, the cross is the only true and legitimate symbol of Christ, apart from the Eucharist itself, which of course commemorates and mediates its saving power. As such it was raised by the Church as the triumphal symbol of its victory over the cruelty and persecution of the Roman Empire; and even taken up by Constantine the Great himself as his palladium, for good or ill: "in this sign, conquer". The cross has, alas, been abused sometimes as a weapon of Christian cultural domination, a provocative sign of something far removed from the lonely death on Calvary. Yet in hospital wards and by bedsides of those sick and dying, it is the supreme symbol of hope and compassion: "in this sign, conquer"; but in a very different way, and to a very different end.

So in the life of a church or chapel, on solemn and high days, at Advent, Christmas, Easter and Pentecost, and also at baptisms and confirmations, the cross will be borne at the head of the clergy and choir, to lead the worship of the church, and to proclaim the centrality of the cross of Christ and his saving power at the heart of any Christian community.

> O Saviour of the world, who by thy Cross and
>   precious blood hast redeemed us:
> Save us and help us, we humbly beseech Thee, O Lord.

Michaelmas

A rumour of angels

"Someone who is often interrupted by other people can seldom sense the presence of angels." This was the considered view of Guthlac, one of the early Anglo-Saxon saints, who lived as a hermit on the small island of Crowland in the Fens in the eighth century, where he died in AD 714. Not much hope for us, then, bombarded by communication, endless visual images, and surrounded by the demands and chatter of other people! Actually, angels impact our lives in hidden and rather oblique ways all the time. As Bonaventure said, they open the shutters of the soul to let in the light of God's reality and love. One way of sensing their presence is to consider moments in life when we may find ourselves alongside them in our common service of God.

The first context is in the care of children. Theophan the Recluse once said: "Of all holy vocations, the care of the young is the holiest." He lived in Russia in the nineteenth century and wrote as a hermit and spiritual director, having been a university professor and then a bishop. The new-born child in particular brings the reality and purity of God very close to us, dispelling for a moment the dark shadows that so often disfigure human lives and behaviour. In the Gospel, Jesus tells us that each child has its guardian angel, to whose patience and self-effacement falls the arduous duty of trying to guide and protect a human being, while not actually manipulating them. In our care of children, we are called to work sensitively with their angels, remembering that the only category of people that Jesus said should have millstones tied round their necks before being dropped in the sea were those who abuse children. On the authority of Jesus, the child stands at the heart of the Church, mediating to us the presence of Christ himself: "for of such are the kingdom of heaven".

The new-born child also alerts us to the reality of the human soul, whose presence almost shines through the fragile beauty of a baby. There is another moment too when the soul can be sharply detected: when a person is dying, and the departure of the soul is imminent. The soul is a mystery; to what extent is it distinct from the person, while being united to it? Bonaventure offers much reflection about the nature and significance of the human soul within the loving purpose of God. For when we pray, we are never alone: not only are our prayers part of the ongoing worship and communion of the Church on earth and in heaven; we also pray with our soul and alongside our guardian angel, and they with us. Thus the words of Jesus take on a further deeper meaning: "where two or three are gathered together in my name, there am I in the midst."

Part of prayer is intercession, and here our prayer unites actively with that of the angels, whose ministry is profoundly intercessory. Through our prayer for others, we are called with them to put love in where love is not. This alerts us to the stream of loving compassion that flows continually from God and is brought to people, often in ways unknown, by angels as messengers of God. In this ministry, humans can have an active share, as Paul indicated, serving as angels of the Lord. One of the privileges of a parish priest is being able to knock on doors unannounced, and very often to be in the right home and family at the right moment, listening to their problems and supporting them in their need. One of the blessings of a monastic community is to be able to offer friendship and kindness to guests, whose time of retreat may be marked by a word spoken in the right way by one of the community. Once again, sensitivity to the needs of other people should alert us to the presence of angels in our midst, and to our common vocation with them as loving servants of the Lord.

Another part of prayer is contemplation, and this surely brings us alongside the angels, whose paramount vocation is the worship of God. There is a delightful story about a hermit in Sinai, who climbed the holy mountain to witness the dawn, as the golden sunlight spread across the numberless summits of pink granite. Suddenly he heard the cry of the angels echoing around and among the mountain peaks: "Holy! Holy! Holy!" We join angels and archangels at the heart of the consecrating prayer of the Eucharist, reciting these solemn and joyful words. Only profound concentration and reverence in worship will alert us to the presence of the angels at this moment around the altar. This is why worship can open the eyes of those without faith and convert them to God, as once happened to a school friend of mine in a Paris church. It is in the worship of God that human beings and angels unite, and we need to seek their help with our private prayers and also in our worship in church.

One of the strongest indicators of our union with the angels in worship is music. Western plainchant has become formalized with great beauty over many centuries. But its root is almost charismatic and certainly contemplative in origin. In the first Life of Dunstan, for example, it is recorded how he learned a chant from an angel in a vision of heaven, which he later dictated to his clergy and monks. Every time Dunstan heard it sung, it moved him to tears, recalling the reality of what he had witnessed. The plainchant setting *Kyrie Rex Splendens* is attributed to him. Certainly in the long night watches in the ancient church at the monastery of Vatopedi on Mount Athos, for example, the cry of the monks as they chant the psalms in Greek conveys the heavenly and spiritual root of the music, which becomes the true language of the soul in worship.

The feast of Michaelmas reminds us that our life, our worship, and our care of other people, is caught up within something much greater than us, a dynamic of divine worship from which flow healing, light and truth, to combat the darkness in the world and to overcome evil: "Holy God, holy and strong, holy and immortal, have mercy upon us!" The ministry of the angels is to form us to become their companions within the eternal love and worship of God, Father, Son and Holy Spirit. Amen.

5 2

Luke the Evangelist

18 October

If you asked someone to name the top stories that Jesus told in the Gospels, they would probably mention those of the Good Samaritan, the Prodigal Son and perhaps the Rich Man and the Beggar. It is an alarming thought that if Luke had not written his Gospel, we would not know these stories at all. Nor would we have the well-loved Christmas stories with which his Gospel opens. Nor would we have the moving and careful description of how the first disciples of Jesus encountered him, risen and alive, walking with them along the road to Emmaus.

If you add to this the fact that the writer of Luke's Gospel also wrote the Acts of the Apostles, he emerges as one of the principal architects of what we now call the New Testament. The history in Acts has been confirmed at various points by archaeology. His method of compiling his Gospel can be examined by comparison with the earlier Gospel of Mark, upon which his narrative rests, and also by seeing how he used material common to his Gospel and that of Matthew, for example the temptations of Jesus. He was a careful and thorough writer, formally commissioned by a wealthy Christian, Theophilus, to collate the various traditions and memories of Jesus in an orderly manner, as he indicates in his preface to the Gospel.

The distinct legacy of Luke is revealed in the considerable number of stories about Jesus that are found only in his Gospel, and also in the way that he relates them. Consider the stories that come from Mary, the mother of Jesus, and her family. Without this testimony, we would know no more than what we find at the start of Matthew's Gospel about the birth of Jesus. Luke recorded the testimony of Mary and her family with great sensitivity and care: he modelled his language on that of the Greek

Old Testament. It was a precious and private tradition that was already well-honed and cherished when he received it. His public presentation of it was also an unusual act of trust, as we find scant mention of the origins of Jesus elsewhere in the New Testament. As a result, Luke has traditionally been seen as the first Christian artist, who painted such vivid word pictures in these stories and elsewhere in his writings.

Luke has also been identified as a doctor and friend of Paul. Certainly the way in which he portrayed Jesus at work among people in need has inspired Christian medical work throughout history until today. He begins his narrative of Jesus' ministry with the unique recollection of an early sermon that Jesus gave in the synagogue of his hometown, Nazareth. Alas, he was not well received there. But the text in Isaiah that Jesus preached about outlined his own agenda as God's Messiah: "The Spirit of the Lord is upon me, for he has anointed me to preach good tidings to the poor, to proclaim release to captives, and recovery of sight to the blind; to set at liberty those who have been crushed, and to proclaim the year of the Lord's favour." What follows in the Gospel demonstrates again and again the deep compassion of Jesus for so many people in need, and his example stands at the heart of Christianity today.

Luke also had great sensitivity to the way in which women responded to Jesus. In Jewish society then it was not customary for rabbis to speak openly with women, let alone to be touched by them. In the case of women of poor moral reputation, or women with certain health problems, there was fear of ritual contamination and moral guilt by association. Jesus broke all such barriers, and there is no finer example of Luke's faithfulness to this memory than in his sensitive portrayal of how a woman whom Jesus had probably already met came in to anoint his feet while he was at dinner with a Pharisee. When challenged by his host, Jesus pronounced the profound truth that "her sins, which were indeed many, are now forgiven, for she loves much; whereas someone for whom little is forgiven shows little love".

Yet there is an austere side to Luke's Gospel as well: it has proved to be a foundation stone of Christian monastic life. Jesus and his immediate disciples sprang from the following of John the Baptist, whose lifestyle in the desert was prominently recorded by Luke. Much of the teaching of John and Jesus in this Gospel is socially challenging and demanding:

"When you give a feast, invite the poor, the maimed, the lame and the blind." Luke's portrayal in Acts of how the first disciples in Jerusalem shared all their possessions and adopted a common life was also fundamental in determining the ethos of later Christian monasticism.

The way in which Luke portrays the death of Jesus on the cross has been crucial for Christianity in its response to persecution and violence from the very beginning: "Father, forgive them; for they know not what they are doing." These words are only in Luke's Gospel. Their significance can be seen in his account of the martyrdom of Stephen in Acts when he prayed: "Lord Jesus, receive my spirit . . . Lord, lay not this sin to their charge." Luke had a clear sense of the purpose of God in the sufferings of Jesus and his followers. His reliance on the suffering servant passages in the prophets and psalms is very evident in his resurrection narrative, as well as throughout Acts. It had its root in the teaching of Jesus himself as recorded in the Gospels.

Luke is outstanding as the first Christian historian, who also had a keen sense of the missionary nature of Christianity and its racially inclusive character. The way in which Peter came to understand that Gentiles as well as Jews were to be included within the life of the Church is recounted in great detail, as is the first known Christian council at Jerusalem to resolve this matter. The conversion of Paul is recounted three times in the Acts of the Apostles, and at one point the narrative is related by the author as "we", implying that he was, for a time, part of the story that he tells.

Finally, we owe to Luke's Gospel three of the first known Christian hymns, which are regularly included in our services at morning and evening prayer: the *Benedictus*, the *Magnificat* and the *Nunc Dimittis*. These beautiful poems, steeped in the language of the Old Testament, are works of spiritual genius that have enriched the worship of Christians from the earliest times. The beginning of the *Gloria in Excelsis* also comes from Luke's Gospel, as the song of the angels at the birth of Jesus. The praise of Luke is thus enshrined in the liturgy as well as in his Gospel, and also in Acts. He has proved to be a great artist and the most eloquent and compassionate of evangelists, and, following in the footsteps of his Master, a true physician of souls.

5 3

All Saints' Day

The origin of the feast of All Saints' Day is an interesting one. In the Orthodox Church, it is still kept on the Sunday after Pentecost. But in the West, it was associated with the consecration of the Pantheon in Rome by Pope Boniface IV to Christian usage in 609–10, and also with a chapel dedicated by Pope Gregory III to All Saints in St Peter's Basilica around the year 733. In 844, its universal observance on 1 November was commanded by Pope Gregory V. This was partly because English missionaries and theologians, led by Alcuin, had promoted the feast across northern Europe as part of the missionary work of the Church. The winter festival of the dead was marked on 1 November among Germanic and Nordic people, as it still is. The feast survived the Reformation in the Church of England because it suited Protestant theology to emphasize the call to all Christians to become saints, to become a holy people. The abolition of saints' days left this feast prominent and also popular. What is its significance today?

Firstly, it is a profoundly ecumenical feast. In the modern Anglican calendar, there are more saints now being commemorated than at any time since the Reformation. You will find Catholic and Orthodox saints commemorated as well as the traditional saints common to all the churches. We also remember those within the Anglican tradition, some of whom were missionary martyrs. In the autumn of 2019, the Roman Catholic Church witnessed the canonization of Cardinal John Henry Newman. The Ecumenical Patriarch of Constantinople also canonized Father Sophrony, the founder of the Orthodox monastery in Essex, along with four recent elders of Mount Athos, whose holy lives of prayer helped to lay the foundation for the recent renewal of monastic life there and in our own country. Saints are still being made, and these both had strong connections with the Church of England.

Secondly, this feast alerts us to the rich inheritance of Christianity. It is highly significant that saints are formed in all parts of the Christian Church as signs of its deep unity in Christ. Today we know far more about the precise historical and social context of many of the saints; their writings are available in reliable editions, and they are no longer symbolical figures confined to stained-glass windows, statues and icons. They were real people whose lives were transformed by the Holy Spirit. Their stories open many windows into history.

What are the hallmarks of a saint? There are three that stand or fall together. Firstly, a saint is a person who makes God real to other people, and especially enables them to sense the reality and love of God as their Father.

Secondly, saints are men and women and sometimes children who have become truly Christ-like in the sense that something of the character of Jesus, his compassion and his suffering may be discerned in them. Many saints have been forged in a crucible of suffering, and the root of Christian veneration of saints lies in the commemoration of martyrs in the early Church. Today there are many Christians being persecuted for their faith, and the twentieth century witnessed the largest numbers of martyrs in Christian history.

Thirdly, a saint is someone in whom the Holy Spirit dwells as hidden fire and light. A saint is someone through whom the fire of the Holy Spirit, his burning love, can spring across into the life of another person or group of people. This is why the testimony of those who knew a saint, or who were influenced and formed in some way by his or her example and spirit, is so important a historical record. A church oblivious to its saints is a church losing its memory and identity.

The root of sanctity lies in martyrdom, and early Christians sensed keenly that when their fellow Christians were killed for their faith something of the mystery of Good Friday and Easter was experienced anew. Their death was a moment of resurrection and that is what was commemorated each year at their tombs in Rome and elsewhere. The other main strand of sanctity lies in the Bible, in the memory of holy men and women like Moses, Elijah and Elisha, John the Baptist, the Virgin

Mary, and also the apostles who were commemorated as martyrs. With the rise of monasticism, the role of holy men and women in the life of the Church, such as Antony or Benedict, became more prominent and defined.

In due time, some of those who led the Church, its bishops, were regarded as saints, either for their courage in the face of persecution, or because of the stature of their spiritual leadership; for example, Ambrose of Milan or Gregory the Great. This tradition has continued until today. Some of the great teachers of the Christian faith have also been canonized—Augustine, Anselm, Aquinas, Bonaventure and Gregory Palamas, also Catherine of Siena, Teresa of Avila and Therese of Lisieux. To their wisdom and clarity of mind the Church owes a great deal, and their writings continue to convey their sanctity and spiritual life. More recently, modern Christians would add those who have been great social reformers, missionaries and pioneers of Christian life in many parts of the world.

There is no need to idealize saints or to turn them into cult figures. They were real human beings, warts and all, and none of them claimed to be perfect. The sheer variety of their characters is testimony to the reality of their existence, however. Nonetheless those closest to them often observed the costly work of divine perfecting in a life totally consecrated to God. They set a standard that summons every Christian today to follow with single-minded dedication the call of Christ, the way of his cross, and the values of his kingdom. To each generation, therefore, the voice of God commands us "to be holy, as I am holy". This is our duty and our joy, for it is our vocation and our heavenly calling.

Other books by Douglas Dales

Living through Dying: The Spiritual Experience of St Paul

Dunstan: Saint and Statesman

Light to the Isles: Mission and Theology in Celtic & Anglo-Saxon Britain

Alcuin: His Life and Legacy

Alcuin: Theology and Thought

Divine Remaking: St Bonaventure and the Gospel of Luke

Way back to God: The Spiritual Theology of St Bonaventure

Truth and Reality: The Wisdom of St Bonaventure

This is my Faith: A Confirmation book

Prayers of our Faith

A Mind Intent on God: The Prayers and Spiritual Writings of Alcuin

Glory: The Spiritual Theology of Michael Ramsey

Glory Descending: Michael Ramsey and His Writings